Masonic Myths and Legends

MASONIC MYTHS AND LEGENDS

PIERRE MOLLIER

Westphalia Press
An Imprint of the Policy Studies Organization
Washington, DC
2022

Westphalia Press
An imprint of Policy Studies Organization
1367 Connecticut Avenue NW
Washington, D.C. 20036
info@ipsonet.org

ISBN: 978-1-63723-828-8

Cover and interior design by Jeffrey Barnes
jbarnesbook.design

Daniel Gutierrez-Sandoval, Executive Director
PSO and Westphalia Press

Updated material and comments on this edition
can be found at the Westphalia Press website:
www.westphaliapress.org

Foreword by Paul Rich vii

I. A 1657– masonic? – Bookplate: *operative* or
   speculative... That is the question? 1

II. A Personal Testimony about Masonry in Britain
    in the Eighteenth Century 5

III. An Archaic "Scottish Master" at the Roots of
     High Degrees 21

IV. Some News from the "Russian Archives" about
    the Early History of the High Degrees: the Scottish
    Order in Berlin from 1742 to 1752 29

V. The Jewish and Christian Sources of the Legend
   of the Vault 39

VI. The Masonic Degree of Rose-Croix and
    Christianity: The Complex Links between Religion
    and Freemasonry during the Enlightenment 45

VII. The 1764 Santo Domingo Manuscript: A
     Reflection of the French Original of the Francken
     Manuscript 61

VIII. Malta, the Knights, and Freemasonry 69

IX. The Stuarts and Freemasonry: The Final Episode 87

X. The Masonic Orders of the Holy Sepulchre in
   Eighteenth-Century France 105

XI. Election, Representation, and Democracy:
    Debates Surrounding the Organization of the
    Grand Orient de France (1773-1789) 123

XII. Theophilanthropy: A (Masonic) Plan for a
     Religion without myths and legends 135

Chapter I has been translated by Jean-Pierre Gonet; other chapters have
been translated and edited by Cadenza Academic Translations.

Pierre Mollier and Masonic Scholarship

A really remarkable aspect of Pierre Mollier's research and publications is that they are more than any one person could possibly do, but they are done by him with such great distinction, all in addition to such yeoman service of many years as the ever obliging librarian of the Grand Orient in Paris and as the inspired director of the Museum of Freemasonry.

Anyone who has ever asked him for guidance with a project will testify to being rewarded by enough leads and hidden closets to explore for a lifetime. Anyone seeking the treasures of Freemasonry is absolutely obliged to visit the museum on Rue Cadet regularly, as he refreshes it frequently. He has helped make Rue Cadet, with its wonderful ambiance, its cafes and groceries and Masons, into an intellectual institution.

He is, in short, an Enlightenment savant who writes profusely about the Enlightenment, as well as its predecessors and its consequences. His footnotes guide us along roads we never knew existed. His enthusiasms are infectious. One hesitates to praise him for fear it will spur him to thirty-hour days. How he combines all his tasks is a deeper secret than the Third Degree.

There are reasons Paris is such an exciting city for Masonic research, and Pierre is one of those reasons. He treats every inquirer, be they a Mason or not, with equal seriousness and respect, whether they are celebrated professors or novice high school history students. No wonder the international conference on masonry and social capital has become the proverbial man who came to dinner and never left. Paris must be its home. Did we say man? Forgive, as women certainly have long been made welcome. In fact, long before other resources in Masonic hands were open to both genders, they have been welcome thanks to Pierre.

Now, put plainly, this book is an invitation to all of us to see what one of the paramount figures in 21st-century fraternal scholarship thinks, not only about the specific subject, but about the place of this research in the general canon of history. There are those who have the erroneous idea that this sort of research is somehow less important because of its subject. Not so; let me relate a personal anecdote.

When I was a callow Harvard undergraduate, far too long ago, I found myself alone in an elevator in Harvard's Widener Library with Arthur Schlesinger Jr., a very famous historian himself and the son of a very famous historian. Seizing the opportunity, I broke the silence by impertinently asking, "Does history prove anything?"

The elevator door opened and as he left me and walked out towards miles of books, he replied, "Little things, little things." I took that and still take it as good advice—intelligent scholarship is like laying bricks, realizing well done and well carefully demarcated topics are the bricks we should lay towards more expansive and far-reaching considerations.

Masonry always needs more specialized studies such as you will find here. Sometimes it has been a house with poorly laid bricks and wild speculation. This book helps to correct such misdirection and lays to rest some ill-founded speculations. It importantly lays foundations for further work. In short, it is an enduring contribution.

Paul Rich
President - Policy Studies Organization,
Westphalia Press

A 1657– Masonic? – bookplate:
operative or *speculative*...
That is the question?

In a previous work, we called masonic bookplates the "Brethren's spiritual coats of arms and marks."[1] We would now like to add a new item to the file, one which raises many questions for the historian of Freemasonry. It is a "typographical" bookplate, i.e., without fine heraldry or specific picture—just a label mentioning the name of the owner of the book. What makes it interesting for us is its date—1657—and the fact that the possessor of the book presents himself as a "Free Mason." Actually, the inscription is "Robert Trollap (of Yorke and Newcastle, Free-Mason) his booke, 1657." Infrequent as it is, this bookplate is well known of British specialists: it can be found on a number of books kept to this day in public or private collections. Why is this date mentioned—a rather unusual practice with bookplates? One can imagine that Trollap wished to take stock of his books in 1657, or even to take a first inventory. But we are, of course, primarily interested in this display of his quality of "Free-Mason," all the more so as it is associated with the old

---

1 *Curiosités Maçonniques. Énigmes, intrigues et secrets dans les Loges*, 2nd edition (Paris, Dervy, 2021), 247.

City of York. What can we know of Robert Trollap?[2] What kind of "Free-Mason" could he be?

He was born in Yorkshire, probably circa 1620, in an old family of York stonecutters. He was a member of the craft himself, received as "Freeman" of the City of York in 1647, although he joined the elite of the construction world by becoming an architect. He mainly worked in Northumberland and Durham. He settled in Gateshead, opposite Newcastle on the other bank of the Tyne. He is known especially for various country manors in the region, as well as for the covered market and the Newcastle Guildhall—the headquarters of corporations, built between 1653 and 1658. In 1660, he adopted the "Palladian style" to build the new manor hall of Eshott and he introduced Baroque elements in the construction of Capheaton Hall in 1667. He was a man of culture: having a plate for one's books shows a special relationship to them. The library at Harvard University—the remote repository of various fields of interest—still has a musical score for viola da gamba by William Lawes which belonged to him.

Perhaps the "Free-Mason" on the bookplate simply refers to his quality as an "operative" Mason. The expression "Freemason," deriving from "Free-stone Mason," that is a Mason who works on a quality of stone particularly adapted to stone cutting, is typically English, while it is, for example, ignored by the Scots. This is all the more interesting as, whereas Newcastle is still in England, the city is quite close to Scotland.

Moreover, the "operative character" of his masonic quality seems to be confirmed by an inscription on a rare threefold carpenter's ruler kept in the National Museum of Scotland in Edinburgh. On one of the folds there is the following engraving: "1655, Robert Trollap of Yorke free mason." The matter would therefore be rather simple. Robert Trollap would have just mentioned his

---

2   Many thanks to my colleague Diane Clements, former Director of the *Library and Museum of Freemasonry* in London, for having set me upon Robert Trollap's trail at the occasion of a discussion about masonic bookplates.

membership in the world of operative Masons by using the English phrase or "Free-Mason."

Some elements, however, incite the historian to inquire further. In fact, the name Trollap also appears in a context which seems more "speculative" than "operative." In 1671, the Bishop (Church of England) of Durham delivered a charter to the "Guild of Freemasons, carvers, stone cutters, brickmakers, glaziers, painters, founders, nailers, etc." of the small town of Gateshead.[3] It was, indeed, upon Trollap's initiative that the charter was requested from the Bishop. It was hoped that by such official recognition and a few privileges, social and economic life could be restored in that small town which had been weakened by the civil war and Cromwell's regime.

Now, out of the five names linked with the "Free-Masons," four, including the Bishop's secretary himself, could not have been "operatives." They were minor notabilities who left their mark in local history and were altogether unconnected with the craft. Therefore, Robert Trollap's rich personality provides a link between operative Freemasonry and the "Accepted masons" of the 17th century. Those English "non-operatives" so well portrayed by Robert Plot in his *Natural History of Staffordshire* in 1686. The bookplate is a testimony of that intermediate and still somewhat mysterious period in the formation of modern Freemasonry. Our Brother Robert Trollap died on December 11, 1686, and had this little quatrain engraved on his stone:

> Here lies Robert Trollup
> Who made yon stones roll up
> When death took his soul up
> His body filled this hole up.

---

3 *Speculative members included in Bishop cosins' charter incorporating the trades of Gateshead, 1671*, AQC. 18, 1905, pp. 53-55.

II

A personal testimony about Masonry in Britain in the eighteenth century

We publish here a rare and exceptionally surprising document. It is the diary of an inquisitive Freemason who reports on his visits to various English, Scottish, and Irish Brothers in around 1780. While the Masonic archives from the eighteenth century may appear relatively substantial, they are mainly administrative in nature. However, "egodocuments," that is to say documents testifying to the Masons' views about their own practices or their understanding of Freemasonry remain quite rare. Hence this exceptionally interesting "excerpt from a traveler's diary," made all the more interesting as this diary is a sort of investigation into British Masonry. It is also palpable when reading between the lines that our traveler saw this as a pilgrimage to the roots of Freemasonry and that he regards his interlocutors as the custodians of "pure and ancient Masonry" who could answer questions asked by Masons who went to investigate on the other side of the Channel.

The document comes from fragments from the archives of the *Philalethes* that the Library of the Grand Orient of France was able to acquire a few years ago. Beginning in the short introduction, reference is also made to the famous *Les Amis Réunis* Lodge, and a "Mr de Langes" is mentioned in the first lines of the diary. This diary is consequently one of the components of the vast investigation undertaken by the Convent held in Paris by the *Philalethes*[1] from the *Les Amis Réunis* Lodge on the origins and nature of Freemasonry.

Two-hundred and thirty years after the *Philalethes,* twenty-first-century Masonic historians can find answers in these pages to topics that still preoccupy them. Back then, and now, one of the major issues in Masonic research was the study of the emergence

---

1   For context, see Charles Porset's reference book, *Les Philalèthes et les Convents de Paris, une politique de la folie.* Paris: Honoré Champion, 1996.

and practice of high degrees. Our diary provides fascinating information about their place in the British Masonry of the 1780s. Information that more or less confirms the intuitions of researchers. In London, "As far as I can judge from what Brother Heseltine told me, the Royal Arch is nothing other than the degree known as "Ecossais" in France; he assures me that there is no going beyond that in England or in Scotland. His grand purpose is to find the true Master's Word and to demonstrate the most essential rays of light to man." And a little further on, he writes, "In England, nothing is known beyond the Royal Arch; its object being the most sublime knowledge of all; it contains all the branches. It has been re-established here." Note that our traveler's interlocutors, although part of the Moderns' Grand Lodge—James Heseltine is in fact its Grand Secretary—hold the Royal Arch in high esteem. Moreover, the "Mr. Brooks" who makes such an impression on our traveler with his Masonic knowledge is probably John Brooks, one of the founders of the Grand and Royal Chapter, the first Grand Chapter of the Royal Arch founded by the Moderns in 1766. As for Scotland: "I was astonished to see that only the craft degrees are known. The Royal Arch is starting to make inroads, but old-fashioned Masons do not pay any attention to it."

This diary is also relevant because it tells us about the views held by these English and Scottish Brothers in the 1780s. The disappointment of our traveler at the very beginning of his investigation, when he meets one of the Grand Lodge of England's most important dignitaries, James Heseltine, is something to savor: "As I discovered, he did not possess the knowledge that it was proper of me to assume he had." Scalded by this initial experience, he no longer aims to meet dignitaries, but "well-informed Masons." Men who, like him and the *Philalethes*, wonder about the origins and nature of Freemasonry. Four characters make appearances and form a singular portrait gallery: Mr. Brooks in London, Brother Spence and Brother Caerny in Edinburgh and, to a lesser extent, Mr. de Valencay, a colonel of engineering in Dublin. The views they discuss in front of our traveler are part of what John Hamill would later call the esoteric-romantic school that is so clearly rooted in the eighteenth century and seems so well represented in Britain. In its early states, the Order drew from the ranks of the Druids, Gnostics, and Benedictines. In around the same time period, we find this type of thought present in the book *The Spirit of Masonry,* published by William Hutchinson in 1775.

Among the revelations collected by our traveler, it is not surprising to discover the famous letter by Henry VI on Freemasonry, the remarkable Leland-Locke manuscript. It is supposedly a Masonic directive written by King Henry VI himself and commented on by the famous philosopher John Locke. We know today that it is fake, a "forgery" to use the vivid English expression. Roger Dachez recounted this curious story in its entirety in the pages of the journal *Renaissance Traditionnelle* a few years ago, in an article entitled: "Un des premiers canulars de l'histoire maçonnique: le manuscrit Leland-Locke (1753)" ["One of the first hoaxes in Masonic history: the Leland-Locke manuscript (1753)"].[2] The manuscript's presence and the importance given to it by our traveler confirm the great influence that it had on British Masonry in the late eighteenth century. In France, it was already known that Jean-Baptiste Willermoz was familiar with it since some texts from the Rectified Scottish Regime refer to it, and we see that the *Philalethes* were also interested in it.

As for the document itself: in what context can it be situated? As its title indicates, it consists of diary excerpts. The diary itself was consequently supposed to be an important text that recounted all the aspects and encounters of our traveler's stay in Britain. Only the passages that are of use to those investigating the Convent of the *Philalethes* have been selected. It will be noted, moreover, that, beyond Masonry, the traveler and the *Philalethes* were also interested in what seemed to fall within the scope of the occult, such as the matter of the peculiar death of Lord Littleton, which had made headlines. We are in the middle of a gothic novel!

We unfortunately do not know who our traveler is. A *Philalethe?* Perhaps—or, in any case, a Mason who is connected and close to them. He quotes Savalette de Langes in the first lines of his testimo-

---

2 *Renaissance Traditionnelle* 97-98 (1994): 87-109.

ny and one gets the impression that Savalette de Langes sent him to Heseltine at the Grand Lodge. Brother Carpentier who wields the pen, despite being the *Philalethes'* "adjutant general," did not leave many traces in the archives. On the other hand, Brother Tiemann who selects the excerpts from the diary and dictates them is well known. He is one of the pillars of the *Philalethes* and Charles Porset has dedicated a substantial biographical note to him.[3]

Ultimately, this document is a testimony—one which must be taken as such and not as an objective description of Masonry in Great Britain in 1780. Thus, everything suggests that there were indeed at the time in England—but perhaps not in London—some degrees "beyond the Royal Arch" such as Knights Templar and even surely a few Rose Croix. This testimony, however, is extremely valuable because it seems authentic and very credible in terms of the general features of British Masonry at this time as perceived by an interested observer.

*** *** ***

Excerpt
from a traveler's diary

The most curious part of this excerpt, and one of the most useful perhaps in the history of this order, is the copy of the questions about the mystery of Masonry, written by King Henry VI. There is no Mason in England, if he is well informed, who has doubted its authenticity for a moment. Its importance led the Grand Or∴ of Eng[land]∴ to include it in the Book of Constitutions. If the A □ R[4] does not already have this constitution, the Brother who is sending this excerpt to him, and who will seek throughout his life to be useful to him and to prove his fraternal attachment to him, offers to bring it to him as a text of interest for the history of the order.

---

3 Porset, *Les Philalèthes*, 612.

4 The *Les Amis Réunis* Lodge.

[other writing]
this excerpt was dictated on [?] same journal to Br∴ Carpentier, adjutant general, by Br∴ Tiemann./.

[F ° 1]

Excerpt from <u>a traveler's</u> diary

London, January 24, 1780.

+ I attended Sommerset's Lodge, the largest and most popular in London. By chance I was introduced by Br ∴ Heseltine, Secrt. of the GO ∴, a man known to Mr. de Langes. As I discovered, he did not possess the knowledge that it was proper for me to assume he had, but I met a Mr. Brooks,[5] a respectable old man who seemed to me to be well informed, having done extensive research, reading the ancient philosophers and everything he could uncover in England with regard to Masonry. He assured me that Masonry has been a known entity at least since the beginning of the fifteenth century. Here are his reasons.

1. In the British Museum there are several missals from this time, and in particular a book containing the Gospels, embellished with all the Masonic symbols. Especially from the third degree. I verified this fact.

2. Wiclef's[6] followers, known as Lollards here, whose leader lived under Edward around 1360, and who were extremely numerous during Henry V's reign, were persecuted for wanting to overthrow

---

5 Of course, there were several Brothers with the name Brooks in London Freemasonry in the 1780s, but the one our traveler encountered is probably John Brooks, one of the founders of the Grand and Royal Chapter in 1766. He then signed the patent founding it as Principal Sojourner. Subsequently, he remained heavily involved in the life of the Grand Chapter and was First Grand Principal twice, in 1771 and 1781. We thank our colleague Martin Cherry, head of the United Grand Library of England, for the research he undertook to identify Brother Brooks.

6 More commonly spelt "Wycliffe," referring to John Wycliffe, the philosopher and Bible translator of the twelfth century.

the government, as history informs us. But the main charges were having a separate religion and being in possession of certain secrets, which, in those superstitious times, made them look dangerous to the state. In Lambeth (the London house belonging to the archbishop of Canterbury), we still see the Lollards' Tower where these unfortunate followers were imprisoned. Many have engraved their names into the stone with knives.

3. Certain questions with answers concerning the mystery of Mas[onry] written by King Henry VI and copied by John Leyland by order of His Majesty.[7] The original version of this curious work is kept in the Bodleian Library. I have a copy. (It is included below on page seven.)

Sir Christ[opher] Wren, the famous archit. of the Church of St Paul is the first to have undertaken a study of Mas[onry] in Engl. He built public lodges. As far as I can judge by what Br ∴ Heseltine told me, the Royal Arch is nothing other than the degree known as "Ecossais" in France; he assures me that no one goes further than that in England or in Scotland. His grand purpose is to find the true Master's Word and to demonstrate to man the most essential rays of light. He did not wish to explain his views about the lodges of Sweden or the Unitarians in Poland—or the doctrine of the Lollards, which he seems to be knowledgeable about.

He told me that the **G.O.A.** [Grand Orient of England] does not recognize the [Rite of] Strict Observance, because its most essential principle does not accord with true Masonry as he demonstrated to the Prince of Mecklenburg that the [Order of] Strict Obs. had worked on his commissions for England a few years ago.

---

7   Like many Masons investigating this time period, our diarist was passionate about the Leland-Locke manuscript, which is unfortunately a forgery. On this strange matter, see Roger Dachez's study: "Un des premiers canulars de l'histoire maçonnique: le manuscrit Leland-Locke (1753)," *Renaissance Traditionnelle* 97-98 (1994): 87-109.

January 30

I did all the research that was possible about what happened to Lord Littleton three days before he died. I have seen people who knew L. very well and who knew about all the peculiarities of the end he met with. I wrote them down before the thing was [F ° 2] published here. I cannot doubt for a moment what follows. Three days before his death, Lord Littleton stayed at the House of Parliament until the wee hours and went to bed quite late. The next morning he suffered violent headaches caused, he said, by a strange thing that had happened to him an hour after he had gone to bed, and which, he added, would leave the deepest impression on his mind if he had a spark of superstition. He woke with a start, saw a bird fluttering around the curtains of his bed, which quickly disappeared. A woman dressed in white had come to him and told him to expect his demise in three days. Recounting the vision, he joked that there was not much time for him to correct the disorder life had brought upon him; however, he was deeply concerned with this thought and went to Epsom on the third day, where he had invited several friends to dinner. About eleven o'clock he said to his friends, "I am doing so well that in an hour I will be able to make fun of my Spirit." Toward midnight, wishing to take off his coat, he was seized by convulsions and died moments later. Another very peculiar situation arose. Lord Littleton had a close friend in Dalford, Kent, who dreamed on the night of his death (Saturday, September 27, 1779) that L. Littleton arrived at his house, entered his bedroom and, as he opened the curtains of his bed, he said to him, "Ah! My dear friend, it's all over; you are seeing me now for the last time."

March 22

I received a letter dated the fifth from the Burren in County Clare, Ireland.

> "Last Thursday when Mr Davoren was having the foundations of an old tower which was near the Abbey of St. Daragh demolished and taken away, he discovered an excavation: twenty-two stairs made of a kind of red granite

that led into a square apartment, carved in a stone of about the same type as the stairs. This room contained fourteen niches in seven of which there were oak boxes laid perpendicularly. They each contained dirt and a skeleton. In the southern part of this room was a square stone with this inscription, written in old Irish:

> Cahil, the son of Rorth: Tieghernam,
> the son of Bracklahur:
> Lunduls, Greanaulin, fardragha
> three brothers.
> illaau, Suilaulin, two sisters.

they drew from the learned Phoenician the spark of life which was extinguished with the sun in the Western Ocean.

(I could not understand this strange inscription until Colonel Valancey informed me in Dublin that Ireland's first residents were a Phoenician colony, that the Irish that is still spoken there is old Phoenician and that it was one of the first European countries that they illuminated with the old light of science).

[F° 3]

Cambridge

March 29

I saw the church called <u>King's Chapel</u>, the most beautiful gothic building I have seen. It is 292 feet long: walls without pillars support this immense vault. The famous archit. Christopher Wren said that he would undertake the construction of such a building if he was shown where to lay the first stone. As history has it, this church was built by Freemasons, who came here as a troop of foreigners; you come in through the southern porch up three steps, from the west by five, and from the north by seven. Above the great door is a sun with the name <u>Jehovah</u> on it. The whole chapel is adorned inside and outside to the tip of the tower with roses and harrows. Under the organs is the figure of an old man hurtling rebellious angels into hell. This piece of sculpture is so admired that one party offered 6000 pounds sterling for it: the chapel was built under King Henry VI. Moreover, it is true that all the Masons who worked at the church of St. Paul in London were admitted to the order by the gd Mr. Wren. This custom is preserved in Scotland, where each apprentice Mason is obliged to become a Freemason.

London

April 5

I spent the morning at Mr. Brooks' in Hammersmith, near London. This is what he said to me:

> "All that I have learned in our history about the science we are dealing with was once in the hands of the Druids here. Caesar employed threats and promises to get them to divulge their knowledge to him. Several monuments attest to this fact. The one recently found at Burren is entirely Druidic; it is of the utmost importance. Henry VI dealt with this kind of research with the Masons who had come to England; they were persecuted shortly thereafter. The scholar <u>John Locke,</u> who did extensive research on Masonry, which is kept in the British Museum, thinks he has found the reason for this persecution. The superstitious population took them for wizards, and this is why the Grand Master's Jewel, which Locke drew there, was the head of a large human figure with horns and a portcullis covering the mouth."

It has been written that the Masons were followers of Basilides in the third century and they professed his erroneous beliefs, Mr. Brooks says there may be a connection. The head of Jupiter-Hammon represented divinity and those familiar with the relationship between nature and science know that the horns are connected to a sign of the zodiac, the piercing eyes express providence, and the portcullis was the emblem of the secret of his secrets that he keeps in his heart. It's pure Druidism. The societies of the Philos. of Lord Clarendon and Cambrid Shive [Cambridgeshire?] were only temporary or short lived; they were busy looking for the science lost during the time of the Troubles and the Horror. In England, nothing is known beyond the Royal Arch, its aim being the most sublime of all knowledge. It contains all the Branches. It was re-established here [F ° 4] in 1764. A friend of Mr. Brooks whom he always called Sir Alexander without ever wanting to tell me his surname, who had been in the East and Constantinople for a long time, was in possession of the secret and the jewels of that degree. He was the one who shared this information with the London lodge.

Oxford April 28

Searching further + (+in the Bodleian Library), in Henry VI's manuscript I saw that Dr. Rawlinson had another one that he attached and from which I copied the following passage:

"The first sparks of light reached man through immediate communication and they passed by tradition from father to son, family to family. All the ancient monuments attest to this truth. The patriarch who brought all the branches of science together was Abraham, the foundation of the light was geometry; it was the first human knowledge and presided over all the rest. Abraham went to Egypt, bringing his Science, but few could enjoy it at first. One of his best disciples was a man named Euclid. It happened during this time [sic] initiation that the great lords of Egypt had so many children, whether legitimate or illegitimate, that it was not possible for them to settle their children into life. Disorder ensued that stoked fears of rebellion. The King promised a handsome reward to whoever proposed the best way to employ and occupy this turbulent generation.

Euclid obtained from the King permission to teach them and to bring them together as a group; he taught them the principles of his science, established order in their society, and employed them in raising those great buildings, of which there are still many today; he established the order of Masonry and prescribed the rules; this was called Geometry. The children of Abraham leaving Egypt went to the land of <u>Bethel</u> called <u>Emencim</u>. King David loved this society very much and gave their chief or master the same authority that Euclid had had in Egypt. Solomon employed them in the construction of the Temple, upheld their old privileges, made new regulations, and promoted order even more than his father had done. These Masons were in possession of Science, separate from the other men. They traveled to several countries to increase their knowledge. Following that, one of their members, a curious and very learned man named <u>Mamon Grecus,</u> who had perfect knowledge of how the Temple was constructed, traveled to France and spread the light there. King Charles Martel welcomed him and gave them a charter. St. Alban came to France, learned about science, brought it back to England, instructed the king (whose confidence he enjoyed), and was made a knight and chief steward. He was the one who doubled the pay of the Masons by giving them three shillings and six pence a week, whereas before they had only received one penny a day. He became England's protomartyr and his martyrdom marks the epoch of science in this country.

Masonry languished under the rule of a foreign king who had invaded the country, until King [F ° 5] Athelstan, having driven out the Danish bandits, restored peace, built many buildings and revived the Royal Art. He had a son named Edwiek [for Edwin] who was extremely protective of the Masons, sent several to other countries to study and procured from his father, the king, another charter and significant privileges; he amassed a large number of Masonic books, in Greek, French, and English. The King then had a scroll or book made that taught how Masonry had been invented, preserved, and expanded. Whenever someone was made a Mason, this scroll was read."

The author of this story adds here: "<u>I personally saw one of these scrolls belonging to Mr. Betzer, a carpenter in Moore-fields</u>." After this historical part come the Rules that the Masons must observe, they relate firstly to morality, secondly to Freemasonry, and thirdly to Operative Masonry. The seventh rule is: you will not sleep with your neighbor's wife. The eighth: you will not sleep with the wife of someone who gives you hospitality.

Edinburgh

May 25

I made the acquaintance of two well-educated Masons: Mr. Spence[8] and Mr. Caerny,[9] both medical doctors. At the beginning of the Reformation and during Cromwell's rule all the ancient monuments and laws and rules were burned, even family and property titles; a law had to be created making forty years of possession a sufficient span of time for a gentleman to secure a piece of land. There were interesting legal documents and books in the abbeys and some proof that science has been cultivated; it has been interrupted in Scotland for nearly 200 years. There are few traditions left here, and the foreigners who used to come here to draw upon the Enlightenment, know much more now, the masters have become the disciples. The last traces had been preserved in Kilwinning Abbey near

---

8   Dr. David Spence, a graduate of the Royal College of Physicians in Edinburgh, published a treatise on obstetrics in 1784, *A System of Midwifery, Theoretical and Practical*. On January 16, 1781, he was made a Fellow of the *Society of the Scottish Antiquaries*. He was initiated into the Canongate Kilwinning Lodge No. 2 on November 29, 1770. We thank our friend Robert Cooper, curator of the Library and Museum of the Grand Lodge of Scotland, for providing us with information on the Masonic affiliations of David Spence and John Cairnie.

9   In connection with the writer James Boswell who quotes him in his diary, Dr. John Cairnie is presented by contemporaries as "a physician who has been active in Jacobite affairs and has traveled extensively on the continent." He seems to have notably resided for a certain length of time in France. He was initiated on May 7, 1755, at the Canongate Kilwinning Lodge No. 2. He died in Edinburgh on May 23, 1791.

Irvine, where there is still a lodge that does not want to recognize the Grand Mastership of Edinburgh, which in return considers it its mother and has the greatest veneration for it. In every meeting here, the third toast is always made to the Mother Lodge of Kilwinning. Nobody is familiar with the Mountain of Heredon here. I saw that everything said about it in France fits the former Kilwinning Abbey. The word M. B. N, which is the master's, is a word in Erse or Phoenician; it means blessing's child; this language is still spoken in northern Scotland and Ireland. The position of Scottish Grand Master was for a series of centuries a hereditary position in the same family; it was the one held by Mr. Sainclair of Roslin.[10] The last of this family renounced this inheritance right in 1736, giving the Masons the freedom to choose a leader; the current one is the Duke of Athole. I was surprised to learn that we only know about the [F ° 6] craft degrees. The Royal Arch is starting to make inroads, but old-fashioned Masons do not pay any attention to it.

May 17

I learned more details from Dr. Caerny about the history of Masonry. We first spoke of the Druids who had been in possession of this science for a long time in Scotland—as in England. These philosophers were first persecuted at the hands of the Romans who wanted to force them to embrace their polytheism; the Scottish and English Kings who had embraced Christianity were even more opposed to them; the Druids then retreated to Wales and the Isle of Anglesey. Troops were sent against them, and they were on the receiving end of the sword blade until no trace was left of them. Their places of worship, where they had separated themselves from the profane, were demolished. They never wrote anything down. What we know about them is the tradition preserved in the northern mountains. MacPherson, Toland, Peyron, and Smith have collected work from this tradition, and the ancient authors, the precious treasures hidden and disfigured by the passage of time. Science was lost here during three different periods. The first, when the Romans

---

10 More commonly spelt "Sinclair of Rosslyn."

wanted to introduce their superstitions and their idolatry. Secondly, during the reign of Edward I. He seized the throne of Scotland, ravaged the country, and transported all the old books to England. I have been assured that there are still several in The Tower's archives. The third: during the Reformation, the fury of the populace was so great that all the convents were pillaged. The civil wars under Charles I completed the destruction of what could have remained. Some sparks from this beautiful fire had been preserved in a Benedictine abbey in Kilwinning. Anticipating that they would sooner or later suffer the fate of the other abbeys, these monks sent their store of knowledge to Rheims in France, which they subsequently decamped to themselves. Before leaving, they communicated the words and signs of Freemasonry to the Kilwinning Masons and since that time it has been the custom here to receive every apprentice Masonic laborer into the order of Freemasons. Those from Kilwinning are still regarded today as the oldest. Edinburgh received its constitution from them, they have their own separate Grand Master, currently the Earl of Eglinton; the names of their officers are found in the great almanac of Edinburgh. The annual public possession [sic: procession] is here on the feast of St. Andrew on November 30; others are sometimes on important occasions. Finally the Grand Master of the Scottish Lodges went on a grand procession to lay the first stone of a building for a public school. There has been a lot of consideration about abolishing the processions, as has been done in London.

Dublin

June 10

I met Mr. de Valencey here, Colonel of Engineering; this man has tremendous knowledge about all things ancient. If ever the Lodge carries out the plan to send a brother on a trip, he must consult Mr. Valencey in particular. He has studied the history of the Phoenicians and the [F ° 7] progress of the sciences in its entirety; he may be extremely useful in the objective we propose. There is another in England who could also be useful: Mr Brooks, member of the Grand Orient. He lives in Hammersmith, six miles from London.

London

When I returned to London I finally procured King Henry VI's Masonic questions. Here is everything related to them. . .

[Here the author of this "Voyage" offers a transcription of this famous apocryphal document. The text is well known]

An Archaic "Scottish Master" at the Roots of High Degrees: The First High Degree Finally Revealed?

Since the eighteenth century, Freemasonry has used a double teaching system, and continues to do so today. Firstly, the Mason moves up through the degrees of Entered Apprentice, Fellowcraft, and Master. However, once they have achieved the Master's degree, those who want to continue their initiatory progression can move up through the high degrees. Although historians have now managed to reconstruct the sources and roots of the first three degrees in Great Britain from the seventeenth century to the 1730s,[1] the origins of "Perfect Master," "Scottish Master," and "Royal Arch" remain rather mysterious. Admittedly, there has been significant progress in the history of the high degrees. They are no longer seen as a late French creation, as was long the case, but as a phenomenon also rooted in the British effervescence of 1717 to 1730, and therefore as coming directly in the wake of the formation of Speculative Freemasonry. Historians such as René Guilly had emphasized that the oldest high degrees—such as the "Royal Arch" (attested in Ireland in 1743) or the "Perfect Master" and the "Scottish Master" (both attested in Paris in 1744)—had points in common and seem to respond to the establishment of the "new" degree of Master in around 1730. Recently, the discovery of two documents has allowed a new model to be proposed for the appearance of the high degrees. At the center of the process lies an archaic degree of "Scottish Master," about which we now have slightly more information. Might it even be the main source for this "Scottish Masonry" that flourished so vigorously in the eighteenth century?

---

1 See Roger Dachez, *Hiram et ses frères: Essai sur les origines du grade de Maître* (Paris: Véga, 2010).

A "Scottish Master" in London in 1733

The first trace of a "Scottish Masonry" in the sense of high degrees (that is, with practices above the degree of Master) is from London in 1733. It tells of the existence of a "Scotts Masons' Lodge," which met in the *Devil's Tavern*, where other Lodges—for example, the *Union Lodge*—also worked. The adjective "Scotts" clearly does not refer to the origin of the Brothers, some of whom we know were already Master Masons. The ceremony of "making and admitting [them as] Scottish Master Masons" therefore gave them an additional degree, distinct from that of "Master Mason." The archives reveal the existence of a few other Scottish Lodges, for example in Bath in 1735. There are therefore several incontestable accounts of a degree of "Scottish Master" being practiced between 1730 and 1740 in England. Bernard Jones, who has devoted a scholarly article to the issue, cites the great English historian Robert F. Gould, "who would have known some of the elements of the ritual" of these first Scottish Master Lodges, and according to whom this ritual was based on "the discovery of the Ineffable Word, lost long ago, in a crypt, by Scottish Crusaders." As with the Masonry of the first three degrees, this "Scottish" Masonry would follow the major currents of exchange, and soon established itself on the continent. Thus, in Paris in 1744, Abbé Pérau stated: "I am well aware that there is a vague rumor among Freemasons, concerning a certain order that they call the Scots, claimed to be superior to ordinary Freemasons & who have their own ceremonies and secrets." However, apart from a few rare and short accounts attesting without doubt to its existence, very little is known about this first degree of "Scottish Master."

An Italian Brother Brings the "Scottish Master" from London to Berlin in 1742

In 2000, the return of a part of the archives of the Grand Orient de France from Russia, which had been pillaged by the Nazis, revealed an essential document for the history of the high degrees: the register (over 150 pages long) of a Lodge of "Scottish Masters" who practiced in Berlin from 1742 to 1749. This very cosmopolitan Lodge was founded by an Italian, Brother Jacopo Fabris, and contained Brothers of various nationalities, many of whom were French. It even carried out its works in French. Yet Fabris, a tireless leader who at the first session received the six other founders of the degree of "Scottish Master," came from London. There he had been a member of the *Union Lodge*, which also met at the *Devil's Tavern*. Moreover, the register reports that the Berlin Brothers were in contact with the London Brothers. Without making hasty connections, we can assume that this "Scottish Master" that Fabris established in Berlin in 1742 was not unrelated to the degree that he may have received in London in the Scotts Masons' Lodge of the Devil's Tavern. He spent some of his evenings in this tavern. An additional element has recently been discovered, justifying the connection between the Scottish Lodges of London and Berlin. In the magnificent Kloss collection of the Grand Orient of the Netherlands, Jan Snoek and Pierre Noël found a mid-1740s copy of the ritual of the Scottish Lodge of Berlin. It clearly corresponds exactly to the words attributed to Gould, because it is based on "the discovery of the Ineffable Word, lost long ago, in a crypt, by Scottish Crusaders." It is therefore highly probable that the "Scottish Masonry" practiced in Berlin in 1742 was the same as that which appeared in London in 1733, and which was used by several "Scotts Masons' Lodges" in England.

Following Jan Snoek and Pierre Noël's discovery, another researcher, Claude Weiler, drew our attention to a unique manuscript that complements and reinforces this hypothesis of a "source" Scottish degree. The unusual nature of the *Copiale* manuscript, discovered in 2011, makes it worthy of a dedicated article of its own. However, here we are very interested in the second, somewhat noncentral part, where the author describes Masonry in his time: around 1745 to 1750. Notably, he devotes several pages to the "Scottish Master." He states that there were two variants: French and German, and he gives many details about both. These elements considerably complete the Kloss manuscript, which although fascinating, remained allusive and even incomplete on several points. It should be noted that the two versions of the "Scottish Master" (the *Copiale* manuscript even proposes a third) show great similarities and are clearly derived from a common source. The author of the *Copiale* manuscript even comments that the Scottish Lodges have "similar, if not identical, ceremonies." When these three documents are examined together, they probably give a fairly representative image of the first high degree of Scottish Master.

A Primitive Form of the Degree of the Royal Arch

I will now attempt to piece together this early Scottish Masonry, much as an archaeologist might restore a large fresco by repositioning various remains of mosaics. In the degree of Master, the legend of Hiram tells us that the true word of the Master was lost when the architect of the Temple died. In the degree of Scottish Master, this true word, which is more substantial because it is the name of God himself, is found again:

> When the Scottish knights were working together to reconstruct the temple of the Almighty in Jerusalem, when they were rebuilding the foundations of the old Temple, this holy place that some call very holy, they found buried there three cubes and three rounded stones, which were the true foundation stones. The knights, who were Masons, went into the greatest ecstasy when they saw under the last stone the word of J or A, which was the true word of the master. They lifted this stone with the greatest care and took it from the holy land on their return to Scotland.

In the remains of the Temple of Solomon during the work to rebuild it, they found buried in the foundations an essential stone bearing the name of God—the true "word of the Master," which had been lost. This is the symbolic theme of the "Royal Arch." Of course, an arch is not yet formally mentioned, but this strange stone certainly has the appearance of a keystone, and it was found in the foundations of the Temple. Following on from Gould's observation, Bernard Jones added that if the elements were confirmed, then "from 1733, the Lodge at the *Devil's Tavern* must have practiced a primitive form of the degree of the Royal Arch." We can now say that this was the case.

The Origins of the Perfect Master

However, this first high degree of "Scottish Master" was symbolically very rich: so rich that it would be divided into several degrees. Thus, alongside the Royal Arch, the "Perfect Master" (one of the first high degrees attested in France) also appeared as a breakaway of the first Scottish Master. The general atmosphere of the Lodge was almost the same: omnipresence of the color green and a systematic use of the symbolic number four (four candlesticks, four trips, and so forth). But above all, the latter element gave the Perfect Master the unique symbol that came to be its mark: a curious motif of four circles in four squares, on top of two columns in a saltire forming a St. Andrew's Cross, with the letter J for Jehovah in the middle. It is worth noting in passing that René Guilly's analysis, which sees this as an emblem of the "Foundation Stone" of Jewish legend, is confirmed by this source document, as the ritual of Scottish Master explains that they are the "true foundation stones." It symbolizes the stone that Yahweh threw into the *Chao* as a foundation for Creation, which Jewish legends place in the depths of the Earth but vertically aligned with the Holy of Holies of the Temple of Jerusalem.

The New Levite "Scottish Master"

After comparing the Kloss manuscript and the descriptions of the ritual in the *Copiale*, we now have quite a precise picture of reception into this first degree of Scottish Master. Candidates to become a Master enter the Scottish Lodge in a position of humility, with a rope around their neck. They must circle the tracing board four times in a silence broken only by the blow of a mallet, and the quiet pronunciation of each of the first three degrees on each circuit. On the fourth circuit, they are purified with water from the basin placed on a small table beside the Bible. The discourse explains that when working in the ruins of the Temple, the Scottish Masters found the ancient word of the Master that had been lost when Hiram died. This word is nothing less than God's true name. The instruction gives the symbolic meaning of the reception:

Q. Where were you received?

A. In the Holy of Holies, under the acacia.

Q. What did you see in the Temple of Solomon?

A. The Ark of the Covenant, and the sea on the twelve cattle.

Q. What is the purpose of the sea?

A. To purify the Levites.

Upon receiving the degree of Scottish Master, the Mason was made a Levite: a preacher serving the Temple, admitted into the Holy of Holies, and put in possession of God's true name! We cannot help but detect a priestly dimension to this first high degree.

The Source of Scottish Masonry

As well as being a direct source for two of the oldest and most important high degrees in Masonic tradition, the "Royal Arch" and the "Perfect Master," our first Scottish Master displays other symbols and legends that recur in many of the high degrees of the eighteenth century, starting with the reference to Knighthood, because it was "Scottish Knights" who found God's true name in the ruins of the Temple during the Crusades. Sometimes at the end of the ceremony, and sometimes several months afterwards, the new Scottish Masters would be dubbed "Knights of the Scottish Order." If, as we think, all of this does come from London, Ramsay did not "invent" the chivalric ancestry of Freemasonry: he really only developed and popularized an idea that was already present in early Speculative Freemasonry. We should remember that the connection with Knighthood is already drafted out in Anderson's *Constitutions* of 1723 and evoked in several British texts from the 1720s.

With the Berlin ritual of "Scottish Master" from 1742 and the explanations given by the *Copiale*, we probably hold one of the most important pieces in the puzzle concerning the origin of the high degrees. However, the images are undeniably unclear, if we take into account the other elements regarding the "high degrees:" the attestation of the Order of Heredom of Kilwinning in London in

1741, the problem of the secret installation of the Master, and quite simply the already very different versions of the degree of Scottish Master in the second half of the 1740s. The *Copiale* tells us that at this time there were the French Scottish Lodge, the Scottish Lodges of Berlin and Brunswick, and "the other Scottish Lodges of Germany." They certainly display many similarities, but also significant differences: the color of the French Scottish Master is not green but red, everything is in threes rather than fours, and so forth.

Perhaps the inconsistencies between these different accounts are the traces of an original practice when the transmission of degrees did not yet take place via a "fully formed," highly structured ceremony. Certain elements would therefore suggest that at the very beginnings of Speculative Freemasonry, the stages of a Mason's career would have been marked by symbolic dialogues, in which the recipient had to participate, around a tracing board placed on a table. This much more flexible form naturally encourages a rapid enriching of the dialogues and commentaries. It is only in a second stage that this symbolic material would have been split into separate and structured ceremonies, with opening, reception, instruction, and closing rituals. This would explain both the deep similarities and the significant differences between the different versions of the rituals, since they did not become fixed in exactly the same way in different Masonic environments. Our first Scottish Masters might therefore have been derived from a great original dialogue on the discovery of the ruins and the reconstruction of the Temple of Jerusalem.

IV
—

Some News from the "Russian Archives" about the Early History of the High Degrees: the Scottish Order in Berlin from 1742 to 1752

The appearance of high degrees, along with their origins, role, and purpose prior to the 1760s, remains one of the most obscure issues in Masonic history. There is little information before 1745, and what does exist is often allusive and always difficult to interpret. The first reference is a list of English lodges dated 1733–1734, which mentions a "Scotch Masons Lodge." The second reference is an excerpt from a Minute Book from the Bath lodge, again in England, recounting that in 1735 brothers were *"admitted and raised to Master Scottish Masons"*[1] In London in 1740, the Minute Book of the Old Lodge no. 1 also records that on June 17, brethren were named "Scottish Master Masons." The next evidence turns up in Paris, where on December 11, 1743, the Grande Loge de France, in article 20 of its *Ordonnances Générales*, warns brethren against what appears to be a new development: *"Having heard recently that some brethren are presenting themselves as Scottish Masters, and in certain lodges, claim rights and privileges..."*[2] Writings from this pe-

---

1 Concerning the questions about the appearance of the high degrees, see: Alain Berheim, "Did Early 'High' or Ecossais Degrees Originate in France?" *Heredom* 5 (1996): 87–113, which presents an extremely clear overview of this complex issue. Concerning the few English documents that refer to "Scott Master Masons" in the 1730s and 1740s, refer to the second section of the article "Earliest evidence of Écossais, 'Scotch' or 'High' degrees" (p. 96). For details concerning these documents, see Eric Ward, "Early Masters' Lodges and Their Relation to Degrees," *A.Q.C.* no. 75 (1962): 131, and in the same batch, the second section of the study "Scots Masters and the Embryo R.A.," pp. 155–181.

2 Ms. Ref XX-239, housed in the G.O. library in the Netherlands, from the Lerouge collection (no. 334), then from the collection of Dr. G. Kloss; present-

riod, such as *L'Ordre des Francs-maçons trahis, Le Parfait Maçon,* and *La Franc-maçonne,* all allude to this "*Secret of Scottish Masons... which is starting to become known in France.*"³ Finally, in 1745, the "*Statutes drawn up by the R.L. St. Jean de Jérusalem*" on June 24 leave no room for doubt, as they state: "*Ordinary Masters will meet with the Irish and Perfect Masters three months after St-John's Day; Elect Masters six months after; Scottish Masters nine months after; and those holding higher degrees when they deem it necessary.*"⁴ With very few documents and with just a few lines at most in each, it is clear that a more complete understanding of this difficult question depends above all on the discovery of new archives.

This underscores the major importance of the work that we will reveal. A logbook from the "*Most Respectable Society of Scottish Masters of the Worshipfull and Most Respectable Union Lodge since its creation on the thirtieth of November, 1742*" has just come to light. It was found in the collection of historical documents in the library of the Grand Orient de France⁵ recently returned by Russia. This is not merely a few lines, but a volume consisting of 140 pages! It is bound in a green hardback binding—21×35 cm—and is in perfect condition. The work—both the paper and ink—seem to be new. There is no difficulty in reading any section of this valuable manuscript. The first 16 sheets contain the "Laws, Statues and Regulations;" in other words, the regulations of the Scottish lodge that have been amended several times over the years. This section is followed by the signatures of nearly 80 masons admitted into the lodge, and who

---

ed, translated and edited by Alain Bernheim, Travaux Villard de Honnecourt no. 17 (1988): 129.

3   "La Parfait Maçon ou les Véritables secrets des quatre grades d'apprentis, Compagnons, Maîtres ordinnaires et Ecossois de la Franche-Maçonnerie," BN Mss FM Baylot Impr. 312; The publication date of 1744 was given by Wolfstieg (bib. no. 29958), as the copyright page indicates only "Imprimé cette année" ("printed this year").

4   BN Mss FM² 362. Discovered and edited by Alain Le Bihan, Franc-Maçons et Ateliers parisiens de la Grande Loge de France au XVIIIé siècle, Paris Bibliothèque Nationale 1973. History and presentation of the document, pp. 391–401.

5   Cote AR/Fonds H pièce 3.

thereby acknowledged their acceptance of these statutes. The next section consists of 141 meetings held by the Scottish lodge from November 30, 1742 to November 13, 1752. The third and final section of the document presents a detailed directory—the civil status of members is often indicated—of brethren who became Scottish Masters during this period. An in-depth study of this exceptional work provides a rich source of information concerning the early years of "Scots Masonry." Historians already had some knowledge of the existence of this Scottish lodge. It was noted in the 6th edition (1903) of the history of the Grand Mother National Lodge of the Three Globes.[6]

The Origins

"The Worshipfull and Most Respectable Scottish Union Lodge" was founded in Berlin on November 30, 1742, by brothers Fabris, Roman, Pérard, Fromery, Roblau, Fünster, and Perret. The capital of the Prussian Empire was in the second year of the promising reign of the young Frederick II, known as Frederick the Great (1712–1740–1786). The first Masonry institution appeared in Prussia on September 13, 1740, with the creation of the lodge called "The Three Globes." As early as 1738, however, Frederick (at the time crown-prince) had been accepted as a Mason by a delegation from a lodge in Hamburg, the first lodge opened in the two German states in 1737. "Scottish" masonry appeared in Prussia two years after the symbolic Masonry that included three degrees.

As Prussia grew increasingly important in Europe, its elite followed the example of their monarch by adopting the French culture as a model. The sovereign greeted French visitors to his capital warmly, and many came to Berlin during this period—Voltaire, for example, was one of the most famous among them. The painter Jacopo Fabris (born in Venice in 1689 and died in Copenhagen in 1771)[7] was a cosmopolitan Italian, while Fünster was probably Ger-

---

6 See Berheim, "Did Early...," p. 100, which gives an English translation of a few lines that the German study devoted to the Scottish Lodge in Berlin.

7 See Bernheim, "Did Early...," p. 100.

man (judging from their names). On this same basis, we can assume that five of the seven founding members were French. Although the majority of brethren who became Scottish Masters during nearly 10 years were German, all the lodge reports were written in French. When signing the statues, some of the new members even Gallicized their first names.

Where did the founders themselves become Scottish Masters and on what basis did they found this new lodge? We do not know. We can only point out that while the Scottish Union lodge was very careful to provide the Scottish lodges it created in different cities with due and proper warrants, the members did not have any founding document in 1742. It seemed to have been created during a meeting as part of a joint project of seven Scottish Masters held on Saint-Andrew's Day in 1742. It is even possible that the new degree was taken to Berlin by a brother, for example the founding Worshipfull Master, Fabris, and that the six other founding Scottish Masters received it only the day before founding the new Scottish lodge. We only have conjectures on this subject.

The Degrees

When the Scottish lodge was created in 1742, it appears to have practiced and transmitted one degree, that of Scottish Master. Indeed, most of the meetings consisted of a vote admitting candidates, then followed by a ceremony conferring the degree to those accepted during the preceding meeting. New members must have received the three symbolic degrees, and those who became Scottish Masters were "Blue" Master Masons. There were therefore no intermediate degrees such as Perfect Master, Irish Master, or Elect Master. Unfortunately, we do not know the Scottish Rite practiced by the Union Lodge. We sincerely regret that we do not have "*Scottish publication in catechism form*"[8] proposed by Brother Roblau[9] on

---

8 f°61.

9 Roblau was a bookseller and was certainly adept at writing. Indeed, we are indebted to him for a "Masonic" edition of *La Consolation philosophique de Boëce, nouvelle traduction avec la vie de l'auteur [...] avec une dédicace masson-*

April 22, 1745, and "*approved by the W. Master and by the entire lodge*," but a certain number of indications in the minutes provide a basis for a general idea. Hence, we learn during a meeting on October 14, 1743, that the regalia are uniformly green, because:

> "*Brother Fünster was responsible for having made the fourteen aprons lined with a green sash and the collars of officers decorated with taffeta of the same colors, that of the Worshipfull Master distinguished by embroidery (?) on the collar.*"[10]

Furthermore, "*the honors of Scottish Masonry [are performed] four by four*" (December 31, 1743), and the Saint-Andrew's cross was one of the chief elements of the degree's symbolism. The color green, the four-by-four acclamation and the Saint-Andrew's cross inevitably bring to mind the "Green Scottish" of the Strict Observance[11] and, in a wider sense, the family of "Scottish Master" rites, of which it is the most representative. It is interesting that Eric Ward suggests that this "Green Scottish" could very well be the English "Scott Master Mason" of the 1730s and 1740s.[12]

---

nique par un frère masson, à Berlin, chez le Frère Roblau, secrétaire de la loge aux trois globes, MVCCXLIV.

10 It is interesting to note that regalia were made for all the brethren of the lodge, which suggests that it was not using specific "Scottish" regalia during the first years of its existence.

11 See Jean-François Var, *La Stricte Observance,* Travaux de la Loge Nationale de Recherche Villard de Honnecourt, series 2, no. 23, G.L.N.F., Paris, 1991. The author procured a transcription of the Green Scottish Rite from the Willermoz collection in the Lyon city library (Ms 5939), p. 97. In it, we read: "The Room is lined with green fabric [...] and illuminated by four candles arranged in a square [...] the aprons are somewhat smaller than those of the Master and lined with green taffeta." The battery is four beats. This text had already been published by Jean Saunier in 1968 in *Le Symbolisme* (no. 385–386): 475–478.

12 Indeed, the rite that he studied in the final section of his article, "An Eighteenth-Century Scots Masters Rituals" (art. cit. p. 162) is clearly a "Green Scottish." The elements that he puts forward in proof of an extremely archaic rite, perhaps those of the famous "Scots Masters Masons," have a certain pertinence, although they are not decisive. The difficult path that he discusses, and which appears to be particularly interesting, should be pursued in depth. The links that exist between the words—accentuated by the translation into

Did this Scottish degree originate in France, as did, in all likelihood, most of the founders of the lodge? This new degree would then be a Masonic manifestation of the French fashion that reigned over Prussia at that time. In contrast, the last signs of activity from the Scottish lodge in Berlin coincide with the change in public opinion toward France and the start of the Seven Year's War that pitted Louis XV against Frederick II.

If this degree of Scottish Master were not French, could it then, like Masonry itself, have come from Britain? The names of certain officers of the Scottish lodge offer some support of this theory. Names such as "Ainé Surveillant" and "Jeune Surveillant" appear to be literal translations of the traditional titles of "Senior Warden" and "Junior Warden" that exist in England—as for the office of the "Stuart de la lodge," the term was probably untranslatable. Could this have been an attempt to legitimize this new degree by suggesting that it had a British origin, which provided it with a certain Masonic authenticity?—especially as the body of the reports uses the terms Premier and Second Surveillants, according to French usage.[13] Another argument supporting the British theory of origin is that the Scottish Union lodge in Berlin was in contact with the Union lodge in London (December 31, 1743).[14] Correspondence with a London lodge would seem to imply that at one time or another there would have been an exchange of information concerning the rites. Especially as Fabris, the founding Worshipfull Master, had himself been initiated in London in this same Union lodge![15]

Up through 1743, when the lodge carried out an initiation, new members were *"admitted Scottish Masters in due and proper form."* Starting with the founding meeting, held on November 30, 1742, the lodge celebrated *"Saint Andrew's Day, the patron saints of the*

French—and slight alterations of meaning from Excellent Maçon, Archimaçon, Maçon de l'Arche on the one hand, and Maçon Parfait on the other, lead naturally to the Maître Parfait.

13 Starting January 29, 1743, f²25.

14 f°43 verso.

15 See Bernheim, "Did Early...", p. 100.

Scots, with all the decorum demanded of such a solemn day."[16] One year later, on November 30, 1743, Saint Andrew's Day was once again the occasion for a particularly important meeting. A ceremony was added to the rites of the lodge; this ceremony appears to have been a significant complement to the degree of Scottish Master. Indeed, after the elections:

> *"The Worshipfull Past Master Brother Fabris raised the New Master in the Chair Brother Roman to a Knight of the Scottish Order by three blows to the back by a sword, while reciting these words: 'I raise and name you Knight of the Scottish Order by these three blows. This first is for the King, the second for the master, the third is for the lodge.' He then gave him the Scottish Order. Finally, the Worshipfull Master who had taken possession of the Chair named Past Master Brothers Fabris, Lamprecht, de Gerresheim, Fromery, Roblau, Fünster, Pérard, D'Alençon, Rollet, de Often and de Brefeld as Knights of said Order, according to the same rites and ceremonies mentioned above. He then pronounced a short speech concerning the duties linked to this Order to which the Secretary replied with a second speech in which he discussed the illustrious history of this Order, its noble progress and its sublimity."[17]*

Where did this knightly ceremony come from? Was it an innovation, and if so, what were its sources and motives? It is as if we are watching the creation of a new degree "live," directly as it happened. It is interesting to note that Brother Fabris named Brother Roman a Scottish knight; this latter then promoted the leading members of the Scottish lodge to this same degree, including the man who, several minutes earlier, had dubbed him. This procedure is hard to interpret within the ways and customs of knighthood, unless it involved an error in the labor or in the report.

Had this rite been kept secret up to this point by the chief found-

---

16 f°21.

17 f°42 verso.

er of the lodge, who would become its first Worshipfull Master, Brother Fabris, who may have considered that after one year in existence, he could finally reveal to the brethren all of the Scottish ceremonies?

It was, in any case, a second knightly degree. It consisted of two fundamental components: the dubbing ceremony and the speech concerning *"the illustrious history of this Order, its noble progress and its sublimity."*[18] Hence, on December 31, 1743, the Master of the Chair *"raised the Most Dignified Brother Katsch—*who had been named a Scottish Master on October 14, 1743—*to Knight of the Scottish Order in due and proper form [... and] Secretary Roblau declared that the Most Dignified Brother Patonnier ardently wished to be initiated into our sublime Scottish Order."*[19] The lodge gave a favorable opinion, so that on the following meeting, held January 23, 1744, *"Secretary Roblau raised [...] the Most Dignified Brother Patonnier to a Scottish Master in due and proper form, then the Worshipfull Master raised this same Brother to a Knight of the Scottish Order in accordance with the customs used during this occasion."*[20] Even though they are always granted one after the other, there were indeed two ceremonial rites practiced in the Scottish Lodge, starting on Saint Andrew's Day in 1743. The Scottish Order was also called the Order of Saint Andrew during the official admittance of *"His Royal Highness Magrave Charles, our Most Illustrious Brother—*on February 13, 1744—*[...] the Worshipfull Master in the Chair Brother Roman, after opening the lodge, received S.A.R. Scottish Master in due and proper form, and Secretary Roblau gave him the explanation of the origins, the words, the signs and marks of the Scottish Master, then the Worshipfull Master presented him with the Order of Saint-Andrew our Patron, which he*

---

18 It is interesting to note that in the oldest versions of the ritual of the Knight of the Orient, the ceremony is equally simple and presents a first sequence during which the new member is dubbed and a second during which he is read the legend of the degree. It is only then that certain passages in the legend of the degree—for example, the crossing of the bridge—is included in the ceremony.

19 f°44.

20 f°44 verso.

accepted."[21] Furthermore, on July 12, 1745, *"Brother Salimbeni suggested to the lodge that from that date on, the members wear the Order of Saint Andrew attached to a wide sash, hanging from the left shoulder to the right side."*[22]

A "Mother Scottish Lodge"?

The Scottish Union lodge did not only set up another type of Masonry in Berlin—it also worked to expand it. A reading of the reports from a meeting held October 28, 1743, reveals that: *"The Most Dignified Brother Fomery notified the lodge that he has opened a Scottish Lodge in Leipzig and that, with the participation of the Most Dignified Brother Perret, they named the Most Dignified Brother, Baron d'Often, Semsch and Gérard de Dresden as Scottish Masters."*[23] Frankfurt followed Leipzig: *"On the 6th of March, 1745, the Most Sublime Scottish Lodge of the Berlin Union granted a warrant to the Most Dignified Scottish Master Brother of the city of Frankfurt-am-Main for the establishment of a Just and Perfect Scottish lodge in this city, under the name of The Sincerity, and declaring by unanimous consent of the brethren mentioned above that the Most Dignified Brethren Stuyrtz be our deputy master of this daughter lodge."*[24] The lodge was set up on September 4, 1745, and, that same day, admitted eight Scottish Masters. This same Brother Strurtz formed Scottish Master centers in Iéna and Erffurth in September and October 1745. This is where a Brother who would play an important role in the history of the upper degrees in Germany became a Scottish Master: *"de Knigge, Gentleman Courlandais, admitted in Iéna on October 8, 1745."*[25] On November 25, 1745, the Union granted a warrant for the creation of a Scottish Lodge in Halle to be called The Concorde, under the direction of Brother Galafrès. On January 11, 1749, the lodge gave a warrant to Brother Neégard "for the creation of a Scottish lodge

---

21 f°46.

22 f°63.

23 f°46.

24 f°123.

25 f°116.

named Four Shining Stars, in the city of Copenhagen.[26] On January 30, 1740, "*the Worshipfull Scottish Union lodge in Berlin, granted to the Most Dignified Brother Seulen, a Transylvanian gentleman, a warrant granting permission to establish a Just and Perfect Scottish Lodge in Transylvania to be called The Four Moons.*"[27] On January 23, 1751, "*The Worshipfull Lodge, on the requisition of His Serene Highness, Brother Louis-Ernest, Duke of Saxe-Gotha, granted him a patent for the establishment of a Scottish Lodge in the city of Altenburg, his residence, under the name of Four Cubic Stones.*"[28]

Given its activism, the Scottish Union lodge appears to have been one of the first Mother Scottish Lodges. It is unique—but is it really so surprising?—to see here that "authentic" and "positive" history supports the Masonic tradition according to which Berlin and the entourage of Frederick II formed one of the oldest centers actively disseminating the "Scottish Rite."

---

26 f°129 verso.

27 f°136.

28 f°128 verso.

V

The Jewish and Christian Sources
of the Legend of the Vault

Whether "Royal Arch" or "Scottish Rite," degrees based on the legend of the Vault play a key role in most Masonic systems. Indeed, they are in all likelihood variants derived from the same English early high degree of "Scots Master." The symbolic framework of these degrees seems likely to have been established in two phases. Firstly, the British "Scots Master"—and its continental equivalent, "Maître Écossais"—were characterized by a legend placing them in the ruins of Solomon's Temple, with the recipient rediscovering—on the ground, under a stone, at the base of a column, but otherwise unspecified—the lost secret of the true name of God. Subsequently—in an almost natural "dramatic" development—this discovery was transferred to a forgotten vault in the Temple's foundations, with the Scot Master developing into the Royal Arch. The practice of continental, and in particular French, Masonry, would go on to bear traces of both developmental strata: thus, in the Ancient and Accepted Scottish Rite, the fifth degree of "Maître Parfait" (Perfect Master) appears to be a French equivalent of the very first Scots Masters, and the thirteenth degree of "Chevalier de Royal Arch" (Knight of the Royal Arch) incorporates the legend of the Vault. In this, however, Freemasonry would appear to have merely adopted and built into the degree system a much older idea that can be found in the esoteric wing of the Judeo-Christian tradition, as sources alluding to the existence of a hidden, secret vault under Solomon's Temple with supposedly divine attributes can be found in both Judaism and Christianity. Looking at these texts in chronological order, I will first refer to a number of Hebrew references that, as far as I am aware, have not previously been considered in connection with this legend, before reviewing the classic sources identified by English masonic historians.

In the Bible

Thought to have been written around 125 BC in Alexandria, in a community of Hellenistic Jews, the Second Book of the Maccabees provides an account of the struggles of the Israelites, and in particular, of course, of the Maccabean Revolt (from 175 to 140 BC) and the martyrdom of the Holy Maccabees. Faced with danger, the servants of the Temple decided to remove its most sacred items in order to protect them from destruction by the Israelites' enemies: Chapter 2, Verse 4[1] explains that:

> The prophet [Jeremias], being warned by God, commanded that the tabernacle and the ark should accompany him, till he came forth to the mountain where Moses went up, and saw the inheritance of God.
>
> And when Jeremias came thither he found a hollow cave: and he carried in thither the tabernacle, and the ark, and the altar of incense, and so stopped the door.
>
> Then some of them that followed him, came up to mark the place: but they could not find it.
>
> And when Jeremias perceived it, he blamed them, saying: "The place shall be unknown, till God gather together the congregation of the people, and receive them to mercy.
>
> And then the Lord will shew these things, and the majesty of the Lord shall appear, and there shall be a cloud as it was also shewed to Moses, and he shewed it when Solomon prayed that the place might be sanctified to the great God."

Here the Ark of the Covenant is therefore hidden on Mount Sinai in a "hollow cave," suggesting a troglodyte or cave dwelling, of which there are many in the Middle East. Other translations also refer to "a chamber in a cave." The door is so well sealed that Jeremi-

---

1 I am grateful to Thomas Dufresne for pointing me to this reference.

as' companions are unable to find the location: it is thus in effect a kind of hidden secret vault, not yet below the Temple, but still in a place with a pivotal role in the history of Israel—Mount Sinai—and secret and sacred since it can only be revealed by theophany. The Second Book of the Maccabees is not included in the Hebrew Bible, but solely in the Catholic and Orthodox canons. It is acknowledged in the Protestant tradition but considered simply to be an interesting intertestamental text.

The Jerusalem Talmud

Also from the Jewish tradition, a passage from the *Shekalim* tractate in the Jerusalem Talmud (c. 400 AD) recounts that:

> [Members] of the household of Rabban Gamaliel and of Rabbi Hananiah the chief of the priests . . . had a tradition from their forefathers that the Ark was hidden there [in the place of the fourteenth prostration]. It once happened that a priest who was busy [there] noticed that the floor [of the wood storage area] was different from the others. He went and told it to his friend but before he had time to finish his words his soul departed. Then they knew for certain that there the Ark was hidden ....
> It is said in the name of Rabbi Oshia that he struck his hammer upon the stone, that it emitted a spark that consumed him.[2]

This Rabbinical tradition is discussed by various exegetes, with the concealment of the Ark underground often attributed to King Josiah. In his fifteenth-century commentary on the Book of Kings, for example, scholar and statesman Isaac Abarbanel (1437–1508) recounts that:

> Solomon knew that the Temple would be destroyed. And so he had a labyrinthine hiding place built under the

---

2   *Mishnah Yomit*, "Mishnah Shekalim," trans. Joshua Kulp, Chapter 6. Available online at: https://www.sefaria.org/Mishnah_Shekalim?lang=bi.

floor of the shrine, and had a stone put there on which he placed the Ark, and also a flask of manna, Aaron's rod, and the anointing oil.[3]

It is no great distance from this "labyrinthine hiding place" to a vault. Even today, some rabbis believe that those who pray at the Wailing Wall do not gather before an archaeological remnant but stand merely a stone's throw from the Ark of the Covenant, still housed "in a labyrinthine hiding place" in the heart of the Temple Mount.

This story also forms part of the Christian tradition, in which it is reported in several books. During the very period in which modern Freemasonry was taking shape, Humphrey Prideaux's influential work *The Old and New Testament Connected in the History of the Jews and Neighbouring Nations* (1717 with numerous subsequent editions; translated into French from 1722), recounted that:

> What became of the old ark, on the destruction of the temple . . . is a dispute among the rabbis. . . . But most of them will have it that King Josiah, being foretold by Huldah the prophetess, that the temple would speedily after his death be destroyed, caused the ark to be put in a vault under ground, which Solomon foreseeing this destruction, had caused of purpose to be built, for the preserving of it.[4]

We see therefore how an unspecified hidden place under the Temple became a "labyrinthine hiding place" and finally a "vault under ground."

---

3   Reference and translation kindly provided by M. Maurice Kriegel, director of studies at the EHESS. I am very grateful to him, and to my friend Jean Passini, for their assistance with this research.

4   Humphrey Prideaux, *The Old and New Testament Connected in the History of the Jews and Neighbouring Nations,* 9th edition (London: Knaplock & Tonson, 1725), Part I, 212.

Philostorgius' *Church History*

The interest of English Masonic historians in the origins of the legend of the Royal Arch naturally goes back a long way.[5] They have identified a Christian source, of which the earliest evidence also dates back to Antiquity, with a Greek author, Philostorgius, describing a hidden vault under the Temple. Philostorgius (c. 370 AD–c. 430 AD) was the author of a *Church History* in twelve books, known to us only through an epitome produced by the Byzantine scholar and patriarch Photius (c. 820–90 AD). Despite being the work of a "heretic"—Philostorgius was an "Arian"—fairly extensive use has been made of this *Church History*, as it recounts numerous episodes in the ancient history of Christianity. Photius' epitome was translated into a French edition published by Louis Cousin in 1676, and includes the episode involving the hidden, secret "Vault." In this account, Emperor Julian (355–363) decided to rebuild the Temple in an effort to invalidate Jesus' prophecy that it would be destroyed forever (Mt 24.2). During the initial work on the foundations, a stone was moved, revealing the entrance to a cave carved out from the rock. A worker fell in and upon feeling around, found a plinth with a scroll placed on top. When he came back up, this was discovered to consist of the first verse of the Prologue to John's Gospel. Here, quite naturally given the Christian context, the discovery no longer concerns the Ark of the Covenant, but rather the book of the New Covenant, and this is in fact the "Legend of the Vault" in the Irish tradition of the Royal Arch. Century after century, the tradition was maintained in certain circles and among religious scholars: first in Protestantism, where a key reference to the legend can be found in Samuel Lee's *Orbis Miraculum, or the Temple of Solomon* (London, 1659), and then in a Catholic context,

---

5   For an overview of the sources of the legend of the Royal Arch identified by English Masonic historians, the reader is referred to two seminal works: Bernard E. Jones on the Royal Arch in *Freemason's Book of the Royal Arch* (London: George G. Harrap & Co, 1957), 126-130, and Harry Carr, *Harry Carr's World of Freemasonry: The Collected Papers and Talks of Harry Carr* (London: Lewis Masonic, 1983), 172-4 and 359.

with three pages dedicated to it in Abbé Fleury's influential *Histoire ecclésiastique* (1724, vol. 4, 89–91): a highly successful work present in all good French libraries in the eighteenth century. Philostorgius' legend was often supplemented by aspects drawn from the work of another ancient author, Ammianus Marcellinus, one of Julian's contemporaries and a committed pagan hostile to Christianity. In his account, during the abortive attempt to rebuild Solomon's Temple, the laborers were also prevented from continuing their work by balls of fire that burst from the foundations and made the place inaccessible (see Ammianus Marcellinus, trans. C. D. Yonge, *Roman History* [London: Bohn, 1862], Book 23; and Fleury, 91). In a Biblical context, "fire is a sign of divine presence and action."[6] The work on the Temple foundations therefore brought about a theophany.

The connection between these religious sources and Masonry is not merely hypothetical, since *Le Nouveau Catéchisme des Francsmaçons, contenant tous les mystères de la maçonnerie,* an exposure from the 1740s, makes explicit reference to the episode (long note on pages 31 and 32) and refers to Abbé Fleury's work.

The origin of this central Masonic legend of a "secret vault"—a hidden, mysterious place, but one open to the divine presence—therefore has deep roots in the oldest "esoteric" ideas of Judaism and Christianity. Furthermore, these important religious sources could have been well known to scholarly Masons in the eighteenth century.

---

6 Marcel Viller, Charles Baumgartner, and André Rayez, *Dictionnaire de spiritualité: Ascétique et mystique, doctrine et histoire* (Beauchesne: Paris, 1964), "Feu," vol. V, 247.

The Masonic Degree of Rose-Croix and Christianity: The Complex Links between Religion and Freemasonry during the Enlightenment

Taking shape starting in 1717, speculative, modern Freemasonry originally practiced the two degrees inherited from operative masonry: "entered apprentice" and "fellow craft"; added to these, in the 1730s, was a third degree called "master." Between then and the 1760s, Freemasons would discover and go about practicing "other degrees." As customary usage has had it, the "other degrees" go by names that are inexact in a literal sense, but now established: "high degrees" or "Scottish degrees." These other degrees were the means by which Freemasonry was to incorporate parts of the symbolic Western corpus, and would be one of the privileged forms of expression of the esoteric and Illuminist currents of the century of the Enlightenment. In the second part of the eighteenth century, the degree of the Knight Rose-Croix would become one of the most esteemed and most practiced of these upper degrees. So, this Masonic ritual raises particularly interesting questions for the historian of ideas about the complex links between Freemasonry and religion.

A Masonic Christian Degree during the Century of the Enlightenment

If the transcription of a document updated by Gustave Bord is to be believed—though it seems to be missing now—the first attestation of the existence of the degree of the "Chevalier Rose-Croix" goes back to the year 1757 and takes place in France. There is a Masonic diploma delivered to Brother Targe by the lodge *Enfants de la Sagesse et Concorde* [*Children of Wisdom and Concord*] on April

9, 1757. One of the signatories, Brother Itéguiemme, follows his paraph with his Masonic attributes: *"ex-maître, substitut A.S.P. Chev. de l'Orient et de Rose-Croix."*[1] The second oldest evidence of this degree's existence is the renowned letter that the Masons of Metz (France) wrote to those in Lyon (France) in June 1761. The object of this valuable message[2] was to exchange information between the order's dignitaries about the degrees known or practiced in the two cities. There it was discovered that the last of the 25 degrees of the Lyon brothers was the *"Chevalier de l'Aigle, du Pélican, Ch^{er} de St André ou maçon d'Heredon"* ["Knight of the Eagle, of the Pelican, K^{nt} of Saint Andrew or Mason of Heredon"] another classic name for the Knight Rose-Croix. It must be noted that the Masons of Metz knew nothing whatsoever about this degree.

Masonic rituals from the eighteenth century with dates are extremely rare. By chance, for the degree of Rose-Croix we have two manuscripts at our disposal bearing dates, 1763 and 1765, which we have no reason to cast doubt upon. The rituals that they offer are moreover widely similar, as is the set of Rose-Croix rituals that can be attributed to the years 1760—1770. Upon reading these texts, the deeply Christian nature of the degree is clearly apparent. The ceremony of the Sovereign Chapter of Rose-Croix successively unfolds in several symbolic places:

> *"The first apartment represents Mount Calvary. It will be covered in black and illuminated by 33 stars"*[3]

> *"The 2nd represents the tomb and the moment of the Resurrection of J.C. It must be decorated as grandly as possible. The wall-covering must be striking, without any human*

---

1   Gustave Bord, *La Franc-Maçonnerie en France des origines à 1815*, Paris, 1908, reprint Slatkine, Geneva-Paris, 1985, p. 538.

2   Transcribed in: Steel-Maret, *Archives Secrètes de la Franc-Maçonnerie*, reprint Slatkine, Geneva-Paris, 1985, 72-78.

3   *Document : un rituel du degré de Rose-Croix daté de 1765*, in *Renaissance Traditionnelle*, année 1971 (n°5, 6 et 7) 73. It is a transcription of manuscript MS 23191, preserved in the archives of the Historical Library [Bibliothèque Historique] of the City of Paris.

figure [...] on the altar, which is well decorated. Jesus C. is represented there leaving the tomb, triumphant."[4]

The Chapter's undertakings open out toward:

"*The instant when the Temple veil ripped, when Shadows and dismay spread over the Earth, when the light grew dark, when the tools of Masonry broke, when the blazing star disappeared, when the cubic stone sweat blood and water, and when the word was lost."*

Then the Wise Master (this is the president's title) makes the following invitation:

"*My brothers, since Masonry is feeling such disgrace, let us give our full attention to new endeavors in order to rediscover the word."[5]*

The candidate to the degree of Rose-Croix does not have marvelous new secrets offered to him right away. He is simply invited to take part in the efforts of disabled knights. The latter group indeed set off seeking "*through one new law to rediscover that word*"[6] that will reestablish order and harmony in the world. At first, the candidate is invited to travel, symbolically, for 33 years. During these peregrinations, he will discover 3 virtues: Faith, Hope, and Charity, which are presented to him as the new foundations of the Order; he is invited to "notice the beauties of this new law."[7]

With serenity restored by these first encouraging discoveries, the candidate is prompted to undertake his quest. He is next led "*into the darkest place where the word must emerge triumphant. [Then] the fruit of his search secures the lost word [for him]."[8]* This word is

---

4   Transcript. cit., R.T. 1971, 75-76.

5   Transcript. cit., R.T. 1971, 156.

6   Transcript. cit., R.T. 1971, 158.

7   Transcript. cit., R.T. 1971, 159.

8   Transcript. cit., R.T. 1971, 162.

revealed to be "*I.N.R.I. or Jesus of Nazareth King of the Jews*"[9] "*the password is Emmanuel.*"[10] Once the reception is brought to an end, the works of the chapter are closed at the

> "*...moment when the word is rediscovered; when the cubic stone is changed into mystic rose, when the blazing star reappears with more splendor; when our tools have regained their forms, when the light is returned with greater radiance, when the darkness is dispersed and when the new law must reign among us and in the labors of perfect masonry.*"[11]

And then, after this is an agape ritual called "Communion Supper" [*Cène*].[12] Around a table covered with a white cloth, the brethren share bread and wine; there are at times along with this, a roasted lamb whose remains will be burned. There must be nothing there but one bread that will be broken; and the brothers must all drink wine from the same cup. For no doubt to remain about the nature of this ceremony, the ritual specifies that it is

> "*...a commemoration of Easter and the appearance of J.C. to his disciples in Emmaus.*"[13]

The set of ceremonies and ritual mechanism of the degree of Sovereign Prince Rose-Croix are therefore performed

> "*...to render allegorically what took place upon the death and upon the resurrection of J.C.*"[14]

So therefore:

> "*The Perfect Mason [...] is the allegory of the redeemer; this*

---

9 Transcript. cit., R.T. 1971, 164.

10 Transcript. cit., R.T. 1971, 165.

11 Transcript. cit., R.T. 1971, 240.

12 Transcript. cit., R.T. 1971, 247.

13 Transcript. cit., R.T. 1971, 241.

14 Transcript. cit., R.T. 1971, 75.

is why it is demanded that all subjects be Christian. The other [degrees] can be given to People who know the old Temple; but the latter can only be given to [those] who are subjected to the new law [...] The principal feast is Holy Thursday."[15]

So it is no surprise to learn that the Rose-Croix ritual of the Marquis de Gages specifies that "*he takes the title of Christian Knight.*"[16]

The profoundly Christian character of the Rose-Croix is all the more important because the degree is presented as the last of the Order, the culmination, the *Nec plus Ultra* of Masonry. This was the case in Lyon in 1761. This is what emerges both from the manuscript of the Marquis de Gages in 1763 as well as from some letters in 1766 from the Comte de Clermont. They are signed, "*Your brother Clermont, Rose Croix parfait Maçon.*"[17] The Grand Master of French Freemasonry, moreover, shows his great interest in this eminent degree. Here he congratulates the Senior Warden of the lodge of the Marquis de Gages, his correspondent, who

> "...*humiliated a very respectable visitor, from the Lodge of the House of the King [la Loge de la Maison du Roy], about all the degrees that he possessed, and refused him the title of Rose-Croix.*"

The Christian nature of the Rose-Croix degree was emphasized from the eighteenth century onwards.

Thus, in 1766, in his book "*L'Etoile Flamboyante*" ["*The Blazing Star*"] the Baron de Tschoudy writes:

> "*The Rose-Croix properly speaking, or Maçon d'Heredon,*

---

15 Transcript. cit., R.T. 1971, 68.

16 BN FM^4 79, f°101 verso.

17 F. Clément, *Contribution à l'Etude des Hauts-Degrees de la Francs-Maçonnerie et particulièrement à l'Histoire du Rite Ecossais Ancien et Accepté en Belgique*, Edition du Sup. Cons. de Belgique, Brussels, 1937. Chap. III, the letters from Grand-Master Clermont are 34-42.

although, all things considered, this is only a renewed Masonry, or Catholicism put into degrees."[18]

Tschoudy returns to this point with several additional details in the secret instruction that he composed for *Les Maîtres Ecossais de Saint-André d'Ecosse*:

> *"The Rose-Croix, in other words Masonry renewed, is nothing other than the Catholic Religion put into degrees. In that respect, it is nevertheless more august in that it depicts objects that are more real, more sacred, more precious; and by combining in one and the same group the consoling mysteries of the Faith & the axioms necessary for salvation, it seems to consecrate the era of those times of grace when our ancestors, sons or nephews of the first Masons, Workers of the first Temple, opened their eyes to the truth, and renounced the prestige of the ancient law to follow the rites of the new, by embracing Christianity during the First Crusade."*[19]

In the early 1780s, the Grand Orient of France entrusted a "Chamber of Degrees" with the task of studying high degrees. On August 20, 1782, the brothers came together to examine the degree of Chevalier Rose-Croix.

> *"The Rf. Dejunquières read the degree entitled Chevalier de l'Aigle - Rose Croix. The chamber judged this degree to have too many Ceremonies in line with ecclesiastical ceremonies and judged that it could not be preserved. It was consequently rejected."*[20]

---

18 [Théodore de Tschoudy], *L'Etoile Flamboyante ou la société des Francs-Maçons considérée sous tous les aspects*, à l'Orient, Chez le silence [1766], 149.

19 [Théodore de Tschoudy], *Ecossois de Saint-André d'Ecosse contenant le développement de l'Art Royal de la Franc-Maçonnerie, & le but direct, essentiel & primitif de son institution...*, in Paris, chez le frère La Vérité, au Grand Globe Français, 1780, 67. In question are manuscripts from Tschoudy published by Labady close to 15 years after the death of the Baron.

20 Registre de la Chambre des Degrees, BN FM[1] 56, f°27.

In the final third of the eighteenth century, the Rose-Croix would become accepted as the terminal degree of Masonry. After hesitation, the team constituting the Grand Chapter General of France would make it the culmination of the four orders, and the rallying of the majority of the chapters to the system adopted by the Grand Orient would therefore contribute to reinforcing the Rose-Croix' eminent position. During the Enlightenment, the Christian nature of the Rose-Croix seems universally admitted. But what Christianity is it a part of? How do we determine, in the vast continent of Judeo-Christian tradition, the Christian current in which this Masonic degree has its roots?

What Christianity for the Chevalier Rose-Croix?

To try to respond to these questions, it is appropriate to examine the ritual's principal sequences in view of the theological conceptions of different schools whose positions have been determined by the controversies that have occupied such a major place in the history of Western Christianity. We are indeed aware of the difficulty of such an undertaking, of the limits and of the necessarily elementary character of the analyses that we are offering, but, as a first step, it means sketching out some hypotheses and opening some workable avenues. Upon ending this journey through the Chevaliers Rose-Croix' abundantly rich ritual, one fact will become obvious: in a century exhausted by theological quarrels—first between Protestants and Catholics, then between "Romans" and Jansenists—the Rose-Croix chapter is the locus of an unheard-of undertaking: restoring primitive worship.

The Theological Virtues

The reception ceremony for the degree of Rose-Croix opens with peregrinations that lead the recipient to discover faith, hope, and charity, or the three theological virtues of the Christian tradition. He is invited to meditate on these virtues that are—he is told—the three pillars of a new law. Etymologically—Theo and Logos—the theological virtues are those that derive from the divine word. In the eighteenth century, each person of course had in mind the classical theology by which everyone was sustained. Even if the force of Thomism had weakened over the course of the centuries, it remained one of the principal structures of Christian dogmatics. Moreover, this conception of the "virtues" had been in part forged by the medieval theology of the "angelic doctor." For Thomas Aquinas, a virtue was a habit that leads to the good. "Habit" must be read not in the everyday and banal sense that the word might have acquired today but in the sense, inherited from Aristotle of "disposition" or "tendency" such as, for example, in the expression "tendency of the spirit." Well within the systematic spirit of the philosophy of the Middle Ages, Thomas Aquinas distinguishes four cardinal or moral virtues: prudence, justice, temperance, and fortitude as well as three theological virtues: *"Faith, hope, and charity are virtues directing us to God [...]I. II. 62 Beyond the virtues that help man to reach his natural end, there are other infused virtues that raise him to his supernatural end: these are theological virtues*[21] *[... They] place the intelligence and will of man in relation with supernatural happiness."*[22] Thus *"Charity is a virtue, because it reaches God by uniting us with him."*[23] If it is by will that man can acquire the moral virtues, on the other hand, his nature is powerless to obtain for him the theological virtues, nature being unable to lead to the supernatural that surpasses it: *"The moral virtues are given by nature [...] the theological virtues, on the contrary, do not come from nature, but from an external principle."*[24] And so *"God gives the theological virtues by supernatural infusion."*[25] It is therefore only by divine grace that man can acquire them; reprising Augustine, these are, Thomas Aquinas explains, *"[virtues] which God works in us without us."*[26] At the end

---

21 Thomas Aquinas, *Summa Theologica*, I[a] II[ae], qu. 62, art. 1. [(Translator's Version: tr. Fathers of the English Dominican Province, *The Summa Theologica of St. Thomas Aquinas*, the Second and Revised Edition, 1920.]

22 Idem, art. 3.

23 Thomas Aquinas, *Summa Theologica*, II[a] II[ae], qu. 23, conclusion.

24 Thomas Aquinas, *Summa Theologica*, I[a], II[ae], qu. 63, art. 1.

25 Idem, art. 3.

26 Idem, art. 4. [see 21 for translator notes]

of their route, since this degree is the *Nec plus Ultra*, despite all their efforts—"confusion slipped into our works"—"the works" of the Masonic Knights are powerless to enable them to rediscover this lost word that will dissipate the Shadows. The new law that will set them on the way, the three virtues that unite with the divine logos, are infused in them by "grace." Analyzed by way of the religious ideas of the 18th century, through that primacy of grace, the ritual of the Rose-Croix clearly leans toward the Reformation (and Jansenism). The Rose-Croix chapter is therefore the locus where is represented "*allegorically what happened upon the death and the resurrection of J.C.*"—an event that, in the Christian tradition, surpasses historic time— and where, under the gaze and by the "grace" of Christ on the cross, the recipient receives "*by divine infusion*" the three virtues by which he "reaches God by uniting us to him." The one who obtains a true knowledge of the three virtues therefore establishes a bridge between the Earth and Heaven—which is the exact definition of the priesthood.

The Imitation of Jesus Christ

Once perfected by the three theological virtues, the recipient must resume the quest for the lost word. For that, he is led "into the darkest place where the word must emerge triumphant." In question is the third level, "*destined to be the image of hell where there will be seven chandeliers bearing large, blazing flames and all the candle holders are heads of the dead and cross-bones. The walls must be covered with a painting of flames and human figures condemned to Hell, which inspires horror and hatred, with chains and people in chains.*"[27] As the ritual specifies, the symbolic passage of the candidate to the deepest abode of the dead is made "*in memory of the nocturnal and mystical journeys that J.[esus] C.[hrist] made in the shadows, which lasted three days.*"[28] "The descent of Christ into Hell"[29] between his

---

27 Description of the third apartment. Document: a ritual from the degree of Rose-Croix dated 1765, *op. cit.*, 77.

28 Document: a ritual from the degree of Rose-Croix dated 1765, *op. cit.*, 162.

29 See for example the commentaries of Thomas Aquinas, "The Descent of

death on the cross and his resurrection the third day is an essential figure of the doctrine of Christian salvation. It is by confronting the forces of Darkness in their kingdom that Jesus triumphs over them and thus delivers man from the anguish of death. This "nocturnal and mystical" visit of Christ to the Underworld may be shown to be particularly welcoming to esotericizing glosses. The Chevalier Rose-Croix is therefore invited to follow the Savior into the Underworld and through this "imitation of Jesus Christ" to also triumph over the horrors of death. It is as an after-result of this supreme test that the lost word will be revealed to him, the word that wrenches him out of the Underworld, disperses the darkness, and brings back the Light even brighter. This word is the name of Jesus, I.N.R.I., Jesus of Nazareth, King of the Jews.

It is difficult to connect this sequence of the ritual to one doctrinal tendency or the other since "The Descent of Christ into the Underworld" is one of the fundamentals of Christianity. The theme appears to be more present in the Churches of the East where it has been the object of a bountiful iconography and numerous commentaries. Less commonly addressed in the Latin tradition, which is moreover peculiar, it nevertheless occupies a definite spot if only because of its position in the *Creed*. In any case, "through their identification with Christ in his passion, they [the Chevaliers Rose-Croix] attain a *priestly* status."[30]

Paradoxically—but the paradox is of course only apparent—this episode of "The Descent of Christ into the Underworld" is both a central figure of Christianity and, in the image of Orpheus, the very archetype of universal initiation that brings life back to a symbolic death in order to then ensure a rebirth leading to another quality of presence in the world. It is certainly one of the figures of Christianity that has the strongest initiatory dimension. It has, besides that, indubitable links with the mysteries of Antiquity.

Christ into the Underworld" *Summa Theologica*, III[a], qu. 52.

30 Jérôme Rousse-Lacordaire, *op. cit.*, 207.

The Communion Supper

Quite obviously, the agape of the Rose-Croix that follows the ceremony emerges as one of the ritual sequences to be analyzed in order
to attribute inspiration of the degree to one current or another of
Christianity and reflect on its priestly dimension. One can say right
away that it would display in the context of Roman Catholicism
a thoroughly blasphemous character. The eucharistic ceremony,
or the holy sacrament since this is what is in question, can only be
conducted by a priest within the framework of mass. Moreover, at
the simple level of vocabulary, in a French context, the word Supper ["Cène" versus "Communion" for Roman Catholics] that is applied to it belongs unambiguously to the Protestant domain.[31] The
sharing of bread and wine among all the Chevaliers Rose-Croix can
also be compared with the Protestant Communion Supper, whereas in that era, in Catholic "communion," consuming the flesh and
blood person of Christ was reserved for the priest alone. In their
passionate debates, the Freemasons, gathered in Paris in 1785 in
the *Convent des Philalèthes* had moreover stressed this: "*The Rose-
Croix, above all, is remarkable for [...] its relation with an essential
ceremony of Lutheran liturgy.*"[32] Connecting the Rose-Croix degree
with Lutheranism this way presents several difficulties, however. Of
course, the rose and the cross are the main features of Luther's coat
of arms. Granted, like all the currents of the Reformation, Lutheranism criticizes the priesthood's clerical monopoly and emphasizes
the universal priesthood to which all men are called. However, on
many points, the ambience that seems to emerge from the Supper of
the Chevaliers Rose-Croix seems closer to Calvinism or to certain
currents of the radical Reformation than to Lutheran positions. It is
probably necessary moreover not to focus on the qualifier "Lutheran" used by the Philalethes. Luther being German and therefore for-

---

31 For this theological analysis of the Rose-Croix ritual, we extensively used André Gounelle's book, *La Cène, sacrement de la division*, Paris, Les Bergers et les
Mages, 1996. The author manages the tour de force of presenting these, to say
the least, austere controversies, in a clear, didactic, and interesting way!

32 Charles Porset, *Les Philalèthes et les Convents de Paris, une politique de la folie*,
Honoré Champion, Paris, 1996, Quatrième circulaire, début 1786, 478.

eign, we should probably see it, in the context of 18th century Paris, as simply a pejorative term in origin, which later came through use to refer to all Protestants.

The description of the Supper of the Chevaliers Rose-Croix is rather short. Can one, however, push the "theological" analysis of the ceremony further? Its very sobriety and the simplicity of its forms seem to exclude every idea of real presence. Moreover, no allusion is made to this. The Communion Supper is, the ritual specifies, "*a commemoration of Easter and the appearance of J.C. to his disciples in Emmaus.*"[33] There again, the words have their importance. Even beyond the debates—famous, if not known—on the real presence, on transubstantiation—situating the Communion Supper of the Rose-Croix in the realm of commemoration places it definitively in the wake of the Reformation and more particularly of Calvinism or the radical Reformation. One of the major controversies between Catholics and Calvinists in 16th- and 17th-century France is the truly sacrificial dimension of the rite of sacrificing bread and wine. In the Catholic holy sacrament, the sacrifice of Jesus is renewed each time for the salvation of the world. For their part, Calvinists want to see it exclusively as commemoration—a very important one, granted—but fortunately only a memorial. In his beautiful work *Une sainte horreur [A Holy Terror]*, Franck Lestringant studies the numerous cases of French Protestants who during the religious wars were to choose martyrdom rather than participate in a Catholic mass where God is once again put to death.[34]

In certain respects, the Supper of the Chevaliers Rose-Croix therefore appears quite inspired by Calvinist, or even radical, theology. Other aspects differentiate it nevertheless and forbid us from only seeing it as "Calvinism put into degrees," to paraphrase Tschoudy. First of all, if all Knights participate equally in the Supper, what is in question, nevertheless, is a secret ceremony. The Calvinist Supper foregrounds the nature of community and the pedagogical testa-

---

33 Document: a ritual from the degree of Rose-Croix dated 1765, *op. cit.*, 241.

34 Frank Lestringant, *Une sainte horreur ou le voyage en Eucharistie XVIᵉ – XVIIIᵉ siècle*, Paris, Presses Universitaires de France, 1996.

ment that the ceremony must have. However, above all, the Supper of the Chevalier Rose-Croix is a silent ceremony whereas the Calvinist Communion Supper only has value as the Word's ritual support, that is to say as reading of and meditation on the Gospel. Practicing a rite without the Word is a heresy.

Taken by the priestly ambience of the ceremony, some Rose-Croix rituals leave silent allegory behind to clearly enter the realm of worship. Thus, in the rituals recently attributed to the Duke of Chartres, perhaps emerging from the leadership circles of the Grand Orient, one discovers, with surprise, an ostensibly liturgical formula: "*The Wise Master takes the bread, breaks off a piece, eats it saying: He took the bread, blessed it, broke it, ate some, and gave it to his disciples!*"[35]

But if the Rose-Croix ceremony displays so many similarities with the Calvinist approach, might it not simply be because both are marked by a will to return to the practices of Ancient Christianity? Another sign of this will to archaism is the act of throwing the leftovers from agape into the fire: this is a direct borrowing from the practices of Jewish Passover.

The Utopia of Original Christianity

The utopia of a return to the simple and authentic forms of original Christianity appears finally to be the project that has underpinned the setting-in-place and regulation of the degree of Rose-Croix. For lack of properly political debates in the 16th, 17th, and 18th centuries, public space was enlivened, to say nothing of being torn apart, by religious controversies, first between Catholics and Protestants, then between Roman and Jansenist Catholics. To support their positions and show their traditional orthodoxy, Protestants, then Jansenists, those contesting Roman authority, would constantly refer to the Original Church. The reference to ancient Christianity and to the original church was one of the major themes to haunt the religious consciousness of Enlightenment man. The beautiful

---

35 *Les rituels du duc de Chartres (1784)*, Editions du Prieuré, 1997, 326.

Histoire Ecclésiastique by l'Abbé Fleury,[36] the great classic on the history of Christianity that was found in all good libraries, presents the first years of the young Christian community in idyllic terms; sincerity and simplicity are its principal traits. In a totally different register, Voltaire himself was a good witness to the sentiments of the upstanding man of the 18th century with regard to the first years of Christianity. At the complete opposite of his attacks against the pomp of the Roman hierarchy as well as against fanaticism and superstition, the patriarch of Fernet describes with emotion, in a style marked by sympathy for the "Original Church," how "the Christians, in early times, took no name other than that of brothers. They assembled and awaited the spirit."[37] As for worship, "the mass was very different [...] in the original church [...] from the time of the apostles, people would assemble in the evening to eat communion, the Lord's supper... (Paul to the Corinthians.[38]) [...] People abided in the breaking of bread..." (Acts, ii: 39) [...] The disciples [had come] together to break bread (Acts, xx 20[39])."[40]

This analytical framework appears all the more credible to us because the Masons of the Enlightenment seem to have been greatly interested in the Primitive Church. During the *Convent des Philalèthes*, brother Baron of Gleichen shows all the similarities between Masonic works and the customs of the "first Christians [who] celebrated their mysteries at night, which they would end like ours, with Agapes [...] it results from this opinion that Masonic science is the science of the true Christian religion, such as was observed by pious Gnostics."[41] And Brother de Paul adds: "To return man to the

---

36 [L'Abbé] Fleury, *Histoire ecclésiastique*, Paris, chez Jean Mariette, 1691, particularly in the first two volumes.

37 Voltaire, *Œuvres complètes*, Tome XVIII, Dictionnaire philosophique, De la primitive Eglise et de ceux qui ont cru la rétablir, 536.

38 I[st] letter to the Corinthians, xi, 20, 33.

39 Verse 7 [c.f. footnote 38].

40 Voltaire, *Œuvres complètes*, Tome XIX, Fragment sur l'histoire générale (1773), Mélanges VIII, 270.

41 Charles Porset, *op. cit.*, Quatrième Circulaire, proponenda IV, mars 1785, 325.

original religion, to the purity and simplicity of his worship, such is the essential nature of Mas.[onic] science."[42] In the same vein, Brother de Raimond declares that: "Mas.[onic] science is the symbol of the true, original religion."[43] This insistence on true religion leaves it of course understood that what one has before one's eyes is false or in any case quite corrupted. In the aftermath of the Convent's work, the Philalèthes would stress that "Several educated M.[asons] find almost identical relations between the generally adopted customs of the interior economy of the M.[asonic] Society, and those whose trace we find in the original Church."[44] The degree of Rose-Croix is certainly one of the most successful attempts to restore original worship and its priesthood.

What is often questioned is the name of Rose-Croix given to this degree. Indeed, the alchemy mobilized by the *Fama Fraternitatis* and the *Confessio* seems quite absent from the original rituals of the Masonic degree of Rose-Croix. But Roland Edighoffer[45] showed that for the author of the manifestos, the young pastor Johann Valentin, it was ultimately only a language and a symbol for defending a theological thesis: reticence before the constitution of a Lutheran orthodoxy and the defense of the spirit of the early Reformation. But under the veil of alchemical allegory, used to avoid the fulmination of the new Lutheran dignitaries, the *ludibrium* of the Rose-Croix would be first of all a plea for a return to the sources of Christianity. Also, not at the surface of things, but in their very substance, Masonic ritual is really inscribed in the true tradition of the Rose-Croix such as it appears at the beginning of the 17th century. In the middle of the 1780s, in the course of the debates of the Convents of Philalethes, the B. of Gleichen had it noted, on the

---

42 Idem.

43 Charles Porset, *op. cit.*, 328.

44 Charles Porset, *op. cit.*, 478.

45 On this question, we will refer to his overview, *Les Rose-Croix*, Collection Que-sais-je? Paris, Presses Universitaires de France, 1986. More widely, on the links between the imagination of Rose-Croix and Freemasonry, we will also consult the chapter *Les Rose-Croix en quête du christianisme primitif* in Jérôme Rousse-Lacordaire, *op. cit.*

topic of the customs of the first Christians, that "sacramental words were secrets: did not real sacramental words experience the fate of the master-word?"[46] True Masonic science therefore overlaps with the priestly art and thus aims to reestablish the true secrets of primitive worship. In the midst of the century of the Enlightenment, the shadow of Melchisedech hovers behind the closed doors of lodges.

---

46 Charles Porset, *op. cit.*, 322.

The 1764 Santo Domingo Manuscript: A Reflection of the French Original of the Francken Manuscript

The "Francken Manuscript" is the reference text for the series of high Masonic degrees that was spread by Henry Andrew Francken (c. 1720–1795) in Jamaica and then on the East Coast of the United States at the end of the eighteenth century. It is therefore an important document on the origins of the Ancient and Accepted Scottish Rite, which is currently the world's most practiced system of high degrees. Francken owed his Masonic system to Étienne (Stephen) Morin, a very active French dignitary in the Caribbean (where there were many French people in the eighteenth century). Morin had received a patent to spread these high degrees in the New World in Paris in 1761, and established them in Santo Domingo (Haiti) between his arrival on the island in January 1763 and his death in 1771. The Masons at the time knew them as the *Masonry of Perfection* or *Order of the Royal Secret*. Since the nineteenth century, historians have adopted the name *Rite of Perfection*.

Nobody doubted that the Francken Manuscript had French sources. In fact, it offers degrees that are shown by all the archives to have developed in France before being exported widely, and particularly into American Masonry by Morin and Francken and via the Antilles. However, the document that I wish to bring to the attention of historians here is much more than a collection of eighteenth-century French high degrees. By its very nature, it shows strong analogies with the Francken Manuscript. Whole sections of the text are identical to that of the Francken Manuscript. This even applies to the errors, such as that stating that Clement VI (not Clement V) was the pope who abolished the Order of the Temple. This document comes from Jean Baylot's collection, and it is now kept in the Masonic section of France's National Library, under the reference "Baylot FM⁴ 15."[1] The specific nature and interest of this document have already been pointed out. In 1972, Paul Naudon identified it as a major source on the Rite of Perfection in the Antilles in the eighteenth century.[2] In 1997, I highlighted its close links to the Francken Manuscript.[3] More recently, Louis Trébuchet has assigned it an important place in the history of the Ancient and Accepted Scottish Rite.[4]

It is a nineteen-centimeter-wide by twenty-one-centimeter-high volume, bound in worn, dark-red Morocco leather. It contains seventy-four folios in laid-paper booklets, though it is difficult to tell how many booklets it contains (there may be four, five, or six of them, of different thicknesses). The watermark is only partially visible, but it seems to show a four beneath a sort of square, scalloped coat of arms featuring a hunting horn and its strap, the two sections of which cross in a gamma shape. At the end of the volume, there are three plates. An introductory note on the Knight of the Sun ritual allows the book to be dated back to 1764, and its origins to be traced to Santo Domingo.

The degree of Knight of the Eagle and of the Sun or the Managed Chaos, final key of the renewed Masonry. Called

1 In issue 2891 of the *Bibliotheca Esoterica* (Dorbon), there is a Masonic manuscript with great similarities to the 1764 manuscript. A happy accident put me in touch with its current owner, who was kind enough to make it available to me. After an in-depth examination, I can state that it is undoubtedly an early nineteenth-century copy of the 1764 Santo Domingo Manuscript.

2 Paul Naudon, "Nouvelles recherches sur les origines du Rite de Perfection," *Travaux Villard de Honnecourt* 7 (1972): 71–76; and Naudon, *Histoire, Rituels, et Tuileur des Hauts-Grades Maçonniques, Le Rite Écossais Ancien et Accepté* (Paris: Dervy-Livres, 1978), presented on page 122 and transcription of an extract on pages 423–427.

3 Pierre Mollier, "Nouvelles Lumières sur la Patente Morin et le Rite de Perfection," *Renaissance Traditionnelle* 110–111 (1997): 125–127 (second publication in *1804–2004 Deux siècles de Rite Écossais Ancien Accepté en France* [Paris: Dervy, 2004]).

4 Louis Trébuchet, *De l'Écosse à l'Écossisme, fondements historiques du Rite Écossais Ancien Accepté*, t.2, *Floraison des grades écossais*, 1: 148–151 and transcription of numerous degrees in vol. 2, 683–931.

*the 21st degree after which the only superior is the Sublime
Order* preceded by the Grand Master Elect who covers it
under the title of Grand Inspector of the Lodges. This degree
was given to me by the Lodge constituted for the Foix Regiment while we were camped by the great river on March
29, 1764 /and to our Lodge to the East of Saint Marc by
Brother Peyrottes/ written at the camp of the great river in
the headland in Santo Domingo in June 1763 [for 1764?].*

We owe the identification of Peyrottes to Alain Bernheim, who
tells us what we can glean from Moreau de Saint-Méry's *Description topographique, physique, civile, politique et historique de la partie française de l'isle Saint-Domingu* (*Topographical, Physical, Civil,
Political, and Historical Description of the French Part of the Island
of Santo Domingo*) (Paris, 1797–1798). Peyrottes was a survey-
or in Saint-Marc in 1750 (page 131) and was appointed general
surveyor of the French part of Santo Domingo on March 6, 1760
(page 102), then replaced in 1768. The last page of our manuscript
ends with the note "to the East of Port-au-Prince, May 9, 1768."
From all of these elements, we can establish that this source came
from a French Mason in Santo Domingo, a soldier who belonged
to the Foix Regiment ("the Lodge constituted for the Foix Regiment while <u>we</u> were camped by the great river") but who later left
it to remain on the island. The "Foix Infantry" was in fact sent to
Santo Domingo in 1760, but they returned to France in July 1765.
It also appears that it was written between 1764 and 1768. A note
at the top of the volume, written at the start of the nineteenth
century, states that:

*This manuscript which is missing four degrees, Apprentice,
Fellow, Master, and the 1ˢᵗ elect or the elect of the 9, was
very probably copied by an officer of the Foix regiment, from
1760 to 1770, who had to do garrison duty with his regiment in Santo Domingo. In particular, it offers the degrees
of the Rite of Heredom or Perfection (in 25 degrees) as seen
in the Convent of Bordeaux in 1762, as well as a very small
number of degrees used in the Ancient and Accepted Scot-*

*tish Rite, which was copied from the above rite and organi-
zed only in 1804.*[5]

Clearly, this note was written at least forty years later than the manuscript. Nevertheless, it was written in a period that is much closer
to the manuscript's era than our own, and above all at a time when
in France, particularly in Paris, there were many people who had
lived in Santo Domingo at the end of the eighteenth century. It
is for all these reasons that I propose to refer to it hereafter as the
"1764 Santo Domingo Manuscript."

It describes the rituals for the degrees of: Secret Master; Perfect
Master; Secret Master by Curiosity or Intimate Secretary; Provost
and Judge or Irish Master; Grand Master Architect; Scottish Trinitarian (Apprentice, Fellow, and Master); Master Elect or Little
Elect; Master Elect of the Fifteen; The Elect of the Twelve—Sub-
lime Elect—Council of the Illustrious Elect; Knight of the Royal
Arch; Patriarch and Knight of the Sun Grand Master of the Light;
Knight of the Lion; Knight of the Orient; Knight of the Orient and
the West Prince of Jerusalem; Grand Master and Venerable of all the
Lodges; Knight of the Eagle and the Pelican; Noachite Knight; sec-
ond degree of Rose-Croix or Clavi Masonry; degrees of Postulant,
Champion, and Great; Sublime Scottish Last Point of Perfection;
Master *ad Vitam* of the Lodges of France and England; Prince of
Jerusalem; Knight of the Royal Axe; Knight of the Eagle and of the
Sun or the Managed Chaos; Grand Inspector of the Lodges Grand
Elect Knight Kadosh; Assembly of the Sublime Princes; Discourse,
Catechism of the Apprentice and Fellow Elect Cohen.

The poor quality of the manuscript, with its generally confused
and rough appearance, cramped writing that is hard to read, terri-
ble use of capitals, crossings out, overcrowding, and multiple cross-
references, probably explains why this document has never been
studied in detail, despite having been known to exist for forty years.

---

5   This comment also shows that at the start of the nineteenth century, Masonic
    contemporaries of the establishment of the Ancient and Accepted Scottish
    Rite in Paris saw the 1764 Santo Domingo manuscript as a founding docu-
    ment for their tradition.

It feels more like a working document, or the personal notes of a dedicated Mason, than a traditional collection of degrees. In any case, it is very different from the well-organized 1783 Francken Manuscript, with its rituals and careful calligraphy, presented in the exact order of the hierarchy of the Rite. Analyzing the 1764 Santo Domingo Manuscript presents many difficulties. Several objections can be made to contest its relationship to the Francken Manuscript. For example, interposed in the traditional scale of the Rite of Perfection are degrees not seen in the Francken Manuscript, such as the "Scottish Trinitarian," the "Patriarch of the Crusades," the "Knight of the Lion," or even, at the end of the work, rituals of the theurgical Order of the Elect Cohens. The traditional degrees of the Rite Perfection sometimes have a significantly different name, which makes their identification somewhat uncertain upon a first reading. Examples include "Master Elect, Little Elect," which is in fact a classic "Elect of the Nine;" or "Elect of the Twelve-Sublime Elect," which is the "Sublime Knight Elect" of the Francken Manuscript. Only an in-depth analysis of the texts reveals the extreme proximity of the 1764 Santo Domingo Manuscript to the Francken Manuscript and to it alone, out of the hundreds of Enlightenment Masonic rituals that can be consulted in the many archival collections today. It caught my attention when I studied the degree of Knight of the Sun; I noticed that in the *corpus* of around fifty eighteenth-century rituals that I had identified only this manuscript had almost the same text as the Francken Manuscript. I then made the same comparisons for the degrees of Secret Master,[6] Knight of the East,[7] and so forth. The results were identical. For the degree of Knight Kadosh,[8] the demonstration is, if possible, even more convincing.

---

6   Pierre Mollier and Jacques Léchelle, "Le Manuscrit Saint-Domingue 1764 à la source du manuscrit Francken—I. Le grade de Maître Secret," *Renaissance Traditionnelle* 113 (1998): 31–45.

7   Pierre Mollier and Jacques Léchelle, "Le Manuscrit Saint-Domingue 1764 à la source du manuscrit Francken—II. Le grade de Chevalier d'Orient," *Renaissance Traditionnelle* 114 (1998): 123–151.

8   Pierre Mollier and Jacques Léchelle, "Le Manuscrit Saint-Domingue 1764 à la source du manuscrit Francken—III. Le grade de Grand Inspecteur Grand Élu

Aside from the positioning of a paragraph spanning a few lines, and two short missing sections, the texts of the rituals in the two works, even though they are around twenty pages long in cramped writing, are exactly the same! In contrast, the twenty or so eighteenth-century Kadosh rituals that I have collected are all significantly or very clearly different. Moreover, only the Knight Kadosh rituals in the 1764 Santo Domingo Manuscript and the Francken Manuscript contain certain extremely characteristic details, such as the notable error stating that Clement VI (rather than Clement V) was the Pope who abolished the Order of the Temple, or a curious list of books on the history of the Templars that the Brothers are invited to consult.

The final element supporting this close link is the presence in the 1764 Santo Domingo Manuscript not (unfortunately) of a complete ritual, but of a text relating to the degree of Prince of the Royal Secret (the first such text known). Folio 69 features a long development entitled "Ralliement des Princes Sublimes" ("Assembly of the Sublime Princes"). As the last page of the manuscript is certified to be from May 9, 1768, we can consider that the degree of the Royal Secret therefore dates back to the period before 1768. The small note at the top of the ritual of the Knight of the Sun takes us back four more years. The Knight of the Sun is described as the "21st degree after which the only superior is the Sublime Order* preceded by the Grand Master Elect who covers it under the title of Grand Inspector of the Lodges." This convoluted wording first gives us the following succession to the top of the system: Knight of the Sun, Grand [Master] Elect Grand Inspector (the traditional name for the Kadosh), and the "Sublime Order*" that the author does not dare name, but which must refer to the "Assembly of the Sublime Princes" described just after the Kadosh ritual in our manuscript.

Yet this comment was "written at the camp of the great river in June 1763 [for 1764]." This shows that the "Royal Secret" existed and was practiced in Santo Domingo in 1764, when Etienne Morin, who a few months before had returned from a long journey, spread his system on the island. In fact, it is my belief that the whole series

---

ou Chevalier Kadosh," *Renaissance Traditionnelle* 120 (1999): 234–277.

of "Scottish" degrees (that is, almost the whole manuscript, which displays a certain unity) was copied in 1764. Only the last few pages on the Elect Cohen were added later, in 1768. This document therefore gives a fixed testimony of the practice of the Rite of Perfection at the time when Etienne Morin implanted it between Santo Domingo and Jamaica. Undoubtedly, it even came from a Brother in his entourage: the presence of the "Royal Secret" (which the copyist did not initially dare to name explicitly) shows that he was allowed into the very heart of Morin's system.

Therefore, the text on the Royal Secret—this "Assembly of the Sublime Princes," which, although not a complete ritual as such, contains all the elements of one—very probably comes from Étienne Morin himself. The magnificent illustration of the "camp of the Princes," which is one of the three plates included in the manuscript, also dates back to 1764. Initially, since it is a very careful piece of work that contrasts with the rough style of the 1764 Santo Domingo Manuscript, I thought that it had been added later on, perhaps even by its owner in the early nineteenth century (the author of the note making the link with the Ancient and Accepted Scottish Rite). However, an in-depth examination of the way the plates have been stuck in at the end of the volume reveals that everything goes together, and that this plate was not a later addition. Importantly (and movingly), its forty-one-centimeter by forty-five-centimeter dimensions and the strong paper chosen suggest that it is probably a real painting that was used in ceremonies.

Is the 1764 Santo Domingo Manuscript the French original from which the Francken Manuscript was copied? No, because if it was, how would we explain the missing sections and the few (admittedly minor, but real) differences between the two documents? It seems more like a testimony on the Rite of Perfection in 1764, and therefore naturally has close links to the French original of the Francken Manuscript. It is even possible to envisage the following hypothesis: the 1764 Santo Domingo Manuscript reflects the state of the Rite of Perfection in 1764, when there were only 23 degrees, as specified in the note at the top of the Knight of the Sun ritual.

This early state might actually help to explain its "rough" aspect. Étienne Morin honed and added to his system between 1764 and 1765–68, when it had 25 degrees, and conferred it to Henry Andrew Francken.

The 1764 Santo Domingo Manuscript therefore appears as a very important document on the beginnings of the Rite of Perfection, and therefore as an essential source on the origins of the Ancient and Accepted Scottish Rite.

Malta, the Knights, and Freemasonry[1]

Formed in London in 1717, over subsequent decades modern Freemasonry spread throughout the whole of eighteenth-century Europe, so quickly and successfully that it still astonishes historians. Its integration and dynamism in Malta, a hub of cultural exchange at the heart of the Mediterranean, is therefore not really surprising, especially given that the young aristocrats who dominated the Order of Saint John (which had many French members) were open to the spirit of their time and particularly to Enlightenment thought. Despite Lodges being condemned by the Pope in 1738, they had many ecclesiastical members in all Catholic countries. The interest of research attempting to improve our understanding of the relationships between Masonry and the Knights of Malta lies not in an apparent paradox (which actually existed not in the eighteenth century), but in the study of the superposition of two networks of sociability, each of which, in its own way, extended over much of Europe. There was a permanent flow of exchange between hundreds of Commanderies of the Order of Saint John in France, Spain, Portugal, Italy, Austria, South Germany—and the Principality of Malta. In all large and medium towns in the kingdoms, the Lodges exchanged "assurances of friendship," welcomed travelling Brothers, corresponded, and cultivated invisible but very real connections throughout Europe. Many young knights were therefore initiated during their period of training in Malta (their "caravans"). Once

1   We wish to thank the *Société de l'Histoire et du Patrimoine de l'Ordre de Malte* (History and Heritage Society of the Order of Malta) and the curator of its archives and its library, Mr. Hugues Lépolard. We are also grateful to our friend Jean-Claude Momal, who helped us with this research and with whom we are working on a prosopography of Freemason Knights of Malta in the eighteenth century, as an extension to this study. Finally, we have drawn significantly on Alain Blondy's excellent book, *L'Ordre de Malte au XVIIIᵉ siècle, des dernières splendeurs à la ruine* (Paris: Bouchène, 2002).

they returned to the continent, they practiced Masonry, thus contributing to the "Universal Republic of Freemasons," in the words of Pierre-Yves Beaurepaire.

Freemasonry in Malta

The First Stones (1730–circa 1750)

Malta appears as one of the first territories in which modern Freemasonry established itself, after Great Britain, the Netherlands, and France. In fact, the first account of the existence of a Lodge on the island dates back to 1730. Shortly before February 14, 1730, the Bailiff of Brandenburg, Philip Guttenburg, made a donation to fund the building of a house for a Masonic Lodge in Msida.[2] Although few traces remain, this early Masonic presence did not escape contemporaries, because in 1740, the inquisitor Ludovico Gualtieri asked Rome what position should be adopted regarding the Freemasons. He was reminded of the 1738 condemnation and invited to pressure the Grand Master of the Order (Raymond Despuig) to publish the *In Eminenti* bull—and to clamp down.[3] The Grand Master then expels the (French) knights Livry,[4] as well as some of his friends for being Freemasons. Despuig died on January 15, 1741. A few months later his successor, Pinto, banished six other knights from the island for attending Masonic meetings.[5] Correspondence

2   Cited by A.J. Aegius, *History of Freemasonry in Malta 1730–1998* (Valletta: Stiges, 1999), 8. The author refers to the following serial number in the Archives of the Order of Saint John, kept in Malta's National Archives: AOM 1187, page 227.

3   AIM, Lettere della Suprema Congregazione, 27 (1739–1783), f°54: "In ordinea quanto Vostra Signoria ha esposto rispetto alla Società dei Liberi Muratori [...] questa Supreme Sagra Congregazione non ha guidicato espediente di trasmetterle altro se non che diversi esemplari della Constitutione Pontifica, con cui la detta società fu gia proibita e condennata [...] Proceda contra quelle persone che usassero tuttavia di fare simili adunanze o ascriversi alla mentovata compagnia," cited in Aegius, *History of Freemasonry in Malta*, 9.

4   It seems there was a significant Masonic hub around Livry from the end of the 1730s. See: Pierre Chevallier, *Le Sceptre, la Crosse et l'Equerre sous Louis XV et Louis XVI 1725–1789* (Paris: Honoré Champion, 1996), 47.

5   *Political State of Great Britain* LIX (1740): 427. Cited by Desmond Cay-

with Rome by the inquisitors Passionei (1743–1754) and then Salviati (1754–1759) shows that the religious authorities often dealt with cases of knights who were Freemason.[6] For example, on September 24, 1757, Cardinal Corsini told the inquisitor Salviati about his suspicions concerning the knights Capons, Somma, Pinto (probably a relative of the Grand Master Serviene), Vaccene, Abela, Grilert, Micallef, Morelli, and Wodworth.[7]

The Lante Trial and the Perfect Harmony *(1756–1776)*

Over a period of around 20 years, there were many incidents demonstrating the presence of Freemasonry in Malta, particularly within the Order of Saint John of Jerusalem. Pushed by the inquisitor, against a background of traditional rivalry between the ecclesiastical authorities and those of the Order, the Grand Master regularly took measures against Freemasons (often the severe penalty of banishment). In April 1776, there was a move from condemnation in principle and ad-hoc measures against individuals to a true official investigation on Freemasonry in Malta, led by the inquisitor Antonio Lante. The investigations began in a charged context, five months after the election of Rohan and seven months after the "priests' revolt." Because of an awareness of the sensitive nature of the subject, the trial took place *in camera* (in relative secrecy). This meticulous police work yielded a highly interesting report[8] on the situation in the 1750s and 1760s. However, very soon, the investigation came to affect everyone, including the inquisitor himself, who was surprised to discover that three of his close circle were Lodge leaders! The ecclesiastical authorities, who had probably supported the initiative as part of their permanent attempts to limit the inde-

wood, "Freemasonry and the Knight of Malta," *Ars Quatuor Coronatorum* 83 (1971): 72.

6   See Aegius, *History of Freemasonry in Malta*, ISSN 10–11.

7   AIM, Corr. 30, f° 309, cited in Aegius, *History of Freemasonry in Malta*, 11.

8   See John Montalto, *The Nobles of Malta 1530–1800* (Malta: Midsea Books Ltd, 1979). John Montalto devotes a whole chapter (XIX-Freemasonry) to describing and analyzing this remarkable document. The serial number of the piece in the Malta Inquisition archives is A.I.M. Ms. Processo Lante.

pendence of the Order, learned that several canons of the Cathedral were Masons. As for Rohan, after just a few months in charge, he had the humiliation of seeing his name cited several times. Not only were there allusions to the Grand Master's Masonry (he was actually initiated to a Lodge in Parma in July 1756), but there were also persistent references to his relative, Prince Camille de Rohan, whose palace in La Valette was one of Malta's most active Masonic centers. The names of many knights, particularly French knights, were revealed. After a few weeks, the inquisition investigators realized they had underestimated the scale of the Masonic phenomenon on the island and in the Order. Finally, following a "regrettable" filing error, the report was "misplaced" and consequently not sent to the Inquisition headquarters in Rome. It was only found 30 years ago, in the Cathedral archives.

One of the main suspects questioned and whose statement is reported was the knight Formosa de Fremeaux. In his interrogation, he explains how he was initiated in 1756, by a Lodge working in Msida. A few days later, he visited another Lodge, led by the knight de Crusyol (Crussol?), who sat in Pawla. Immediately, Formosa de Fremeaux appeared as a highly zealous Mason. He admitted to having had Masonic symbols painted in his house in Zejtun and to hosting a Lodge in his La Valette residence to receive the knight Guasconi, who had come especially from Palermo to be initiated. He gives quite a detailed description of the Masonic ceremonies. From the details he presents, it is clear that the Maltese Masons practiced the Masonic Rite that was used in France at the time, today called the "French Rite." Moreover, the charter of the third Lodge cited in the Lante report came from France. On February 13, 1766, in Toulon, Brother Beufier de la Louerie gave the knight Lincel a warrant to create a Lodge in Malta, with the distinctive name of the *Perfect Harmony*. Lincel delegated his warrant to another knight, who would be an active Mason until the end of the century: Ligondès, colonel of the Maltese regiment then chamberlain to the Grand Master. A formerly unknown account confirms and completes the documentation on the Lante trial. It was found in the travel journals of a young German aristocrat: Karl von Zinzendorf.[9] His journal indicates that he was received as a Mason in Malta in March 1766. The Lodge had by then changed its distinctive name slightly, to become *Saint John of Scotland of Secrecy and Harmony*, daughter of Marseille's *Saint John of Scotland*. The name stuck. In his journal on Malta, he also names other members of the Lodge, who like himself were Knights of Malta: Ligondès, Crose-Lincel (the two signatories of the license) Tommasi, Loras, Litta, Guillet de Monthouxanf, and the Prince of Caramanico's younger Brother, the Count of Aquino who accompanied Cagliostro during his stays in Naples, Malta, and Sicily. Most of these names recur later on.

Saint John's Lodge of Secrecy and Harmony (1788–1792)

After the Lante report, the other main source for the history of Freemasonry in Malta is the file sent to the Grand Lodge of England by a group of Masons, to place under its Obedience their newly recreated Lodge with the distinctive name *Saint John's Lodge of Secrecy and Harmony*. Once again, the documents describe the situation at the time of writing (around 1790), but by citing various Masonic antecedents, they give a great deal of information about the two preceding decades. Moreover, these were internal Masonic documents, so are much more precise concerning the names and masonic careers of the Brothers. Overall, this correspondence with London confirms the picture we have painted so far. The Masons of Malta write that:

> *From the start of the century, our Masonic association under the distinctive name of Harmony and Secrecy embraced and professed all the degrees of symbolic Masonry. Afterwards, in around 1764, our Brothers reunited under the Doctrine of the Lodges of Saint John of Scotland by affiliation with that of Marseille; from then on we remained*

9 Christine Lebeau studied the Zinzendorf Brothers outside of the Masonic context, in her thesis entitled *Aristocrates et grands commis à la cour de Vienne (1748–1791). Le modèle français* (Paris: CNRS, 1996). Our thanks to Pierre-Yves Beaurepaire, who directed us to this reference discovered by Helmut Watzlawick during his work on the publication of Zinzendorf's travel journals.

custodians of the instructions and symbolic rituals up to the three Scottish Degrees, to which those of Knight of the Orient and Knight of the Sun and the Rosy Cross were joined by moral analogy or some other inclination. We preserve these various instructions in their entirety, and, moreover, some of the members [...] are decorated with the High Degrees of foreign or French Masonry.[10]

Thus, the Maltese Masons used a typical eighteenth-century French Masonic structure. After the traditional Degrees of Apprentice, Fellow, and Master, the Brothers used a series of those high degrees that were the privileged channels of esotericism and the chivalric imagination in the century of Enlightenment. These rituals were particularly fashionable in the Lodges of southern France, particularly in Toulon, or around *Saint John of Scotland* in Marseille. Thus, the Knight of the Sun uses an astonishing alchemical symbolism concerning the Rosy Cross, which appears as an attempt to restore primitive Christianity by emphasizing its "initiatory" dimension. The Maltese Brothers explain the circumstances leading them to revive a Lodge which had not met for several years:

We, the undersigned Master, Fellow, and Apprentice Brothers, some from the old Maltese Lodge known as Saint John's Lodge of Secrecy and Harmony, some from other Lodges and under various systems.

Regretfully long separated from the whole association and from Masonic work, but wishing to be reintegrated into the ancient practice of a wise and holy rule whose foundations and character will never be erased from our memory, we have eagerly seized the opportunity of the visit from the Very

---

10 Translated from: Library-Archives of the United Grand Lodge of England, File on Saint John's Lodge of Secrecy and Harmony, serial number 1136, item 20/D/6, f°2: "Lettre adressée par les Frères de Malte à la Grande Loge – des 'Moderns' – à Londres, le 24 avril 1792." The original letter from the Brothers of Malta to the Grand Lodge of the "moderns" in London on April 24, 1792, is in French.

Reverend Brother Count von Kolowrat, current chamber-lain to H.M. the Emperor to resume our old practices under his leadership.[11]

This letter is particularly interesting, because for the first time it gives the full list of the members of a Maltese Lodge. This shows how deeply Masonry was present at the heart of the Order of Saint John of Jerusalem. The seven founders were all knights. The list features many known names who had meanwhile progressed within the Order, with three becoming Great Crosses: Abel de Loras, then a pillar of the *Langue d'Auvergne* and a member of Grand Master Rohan's close circle, the bailiff Tommasi, former page to Pinto who became Grand Master during the difficult period of the early nineteenth century, and Count de Litta. Kolowrat was Grand Prior of Bohemia and one of Rohan's key men for relations with central Europe. Many members of the Lodge were not just knights: they were dignitaries of the Order. Thirty years later, Formosa de Fremeaux was still on board, and was joined by Ligondès, who even became Worshipful Master (president) in 1790. Because of the atmosphere of growing confusion at the start of the 1790s, the Lodge became a gathering point for Masons, with around 40 Brothers. Over two thirds were knights of Saint John of Jerusalem; the others were either priests or often important employees of the Order, such as Doublet, who was secretary to the Grand Master. Although he was a Mason, there is no proof that Rohan participated in the works of *Saint John's Lodge of Secrecy and Harmony*. It is even very probable that he abstained, because of his position. However, several clues indicate that he was relatively sympathetic or at least benevolently neutral towards the Lodge.[12] Although he warns against hasty conclusions, Alain Blondy notes that *"the vast majority of knights who*

---

11 Translated from: Library-Archives of the United Grand Lodge of England, File on Saint John's Lodge of Secrecy and Harmony, serial number 1136, item 20/D/2. Letter of June 30, 1788.

12 There are two types of evidence for this: the ill will with which he followed repeated orders from the Holy See and from the Inquisition to crack down on the Masons, and the shining careers of most Lodge members within the Order.

in one way or another held very important roles under Rohan's princedom, belonged to Masonry."[13]

The Knights of Malta: a European Masonic Network

Masonry connects Malta to the European Capitals

Although Freemasonry saw a certain success on the island throughout the eighteenth century and in Saint John of Jerusalem, it was also a part of the link between Malta and the different power centers in Europe. The knights travelled extensively. When they were young, they left the land of their birth to complete their "caravans" and spend at least the required period in Malta. Following this, their career in the Order brought them back to the continent to take charge of a Commanderie in France, Italy, Spain, Austria, etc. However, they regularly returned to the island to defend their interests at headquarters and obtain a more important role or position. Not to mention the Order's diplomatic staff in the various Catholic courts and the knights employed for a period in the national navies either in the headquarters or the major ports. There were far more knights of Malta across Europe than there were on the island. The knights' cosmopolitanism, which even became a sort of literary type, inevitably met that of Freemasonry. In fact, by their very nature, the Lodges (particularly in the eighteenth century) were a place of contact and exchange of "commerce" in the old sense of the word. This vocation defined the first article of the founding text of modern Freemasonry, Anderson's *Constitutions* (1723): "*Masonry becomes the Center of the Union, and the Means of conciliating true Friendship among Persons that must else have remain'd at a perpetual Distance.*" The Brothers (of Malta!) of the Chevalier des Grieux must have been familiar with this precept repeated by the follower of another cult (though his type of devotions was not all that foreign to many "men of the Religion"):[14] Casanova, who explains in his *Mémoires*:

---

13 Translated from Alain Blondy, *L'Ordre de Malte au XVIIIe siècle*, 274.

14 Jean Potocki, who knew Malta well, having been received as a knight there in 1778 and stayed there for some time, gave the following words to one of the heroes in his extraordinary novel *The Manuscript Found in Saragossa*: "I en-

Every young man who travels, who wants to know the wide
world, who does not want to be inferior to another and ex-
cluded from the company of his equals in our times, must be
initiated into what we call Freemasonry.[15]

Infused with the contemporary idea of the unity of humanity
and with their aspiration to the utopia of a universal Brotherhood,
Enlightenment thinkers scrupulously made connections with Freemasons in other towns and countries. The itinerant lifestyle of the
knight Brothers meant they were inevitably very sensitive to this
concept.

There were continuous Masonic links between Malta and the
major French ports of the Mediterranean: Toulon and Marseille.
From 1760 to 1780, the knights of Ligondès, Le Boscage, Vinti-
mille, Seillons, La Tour du Pin, Pontévès, and Chabriant carried
out Masonic works between Toulon and Malta.[16] In the same period, the Lodges of Marseille, with *Saint John of Scotland* at the
forefront, regularly had commanders from Malta within their
ranks: La Durane de Piolin, Hana, Vincencini[17] Foresta, and Vilhe-

---

tered Malta before leaving childhood [...], so I could and still can have a claim
to the first Dignities of the Order. However, since these are accessed only later
in life, and I had nothing to do in the meantime, I followed the example of our
first bailiffs, who perhaps should have set me a better one. In a word, I spent
my time making love." Translated from the French in René Radrizzani, *Histoire du commandeur de Toralva* (Paris: Edition José Corti, 1990), 535. Our
thanks to Pierre Lachkareff for pointing out this rich reference to us. On this
image in literature, it is also useful to consult Claire Eliane Engel's writings on
their place in the Abbé Prévost's novels. See *Les Chevaliers de Malte* (Paris: Les
Presses contemporaines, 1972), 249–253.

15 Translated from Charles Porset, "Casanova Franc-maçon," *Chroniques d'Histoire maçonnique* 49 (1998): 5.

16 *Tableau général des Frères qui composent la R∴ Loge de St. Jean de la Marine,
sous le titre distinctif de la Parfaite Harmonie, constituée à l'Orient de Toulon le
20 avril 1764, arrêté le 14 mars 5785 [1785].* ("List of the Brothers of the *St.
Jean de la Marine* Lodge, under the distinctive title of the Perfect Harmony,
formed in the Orient of Toulon on April 20, 1764, stopped on March 14,
5785 [1785].")

17 Jacques Choisey, *La Respectable Loge de Saint Jean d'Ecosse, Mère Loge Ecos-*

na.[18] As for Torring, a young Apprentice of the Lodge, he was "in Malta." The most unusual case preserved in the annals is that of the Lodge of Narbonne, led by the Chefdebien d'Armissan family. The oldest son was initiated in Malta during his "caravans," and when he returned to Narbonne, he created a Lodge there with his Brothers (the baron, abbot, and knights of Chefdebien). There were no less than 13 knights of Malta among the lodge's 48 members.[19] Chefdebien was a passionate Mason in contact with his cousin d'Aigrefeuille, who himself corresponded with those Brothers most informed about the Mysteries of the (Masonic) Order in Paris, Lyon, and even Germany. Alain Blondy also describes the case of *Saint John of Jerusalem*,[20] who from Saône to Rhône gathered several knights around the commander Tulle de Villefranche, to the extent that the Lyon Brothers simply called the group "the Malta Lodge."[21] On December 13, 1766, the young knight Karl von Zinzendorf, who we left as a Mason in Malta, was in Strasbourg. He was participating in the work of the *Candeur* Lodge, to which he was introduced by another knight of Saint John of Jerusalem, Brother Flachslanden, second warden of the lodge.[22] *La Candeur* was a real nerve-center for links with Germany and central Europe.[23]

---

saise à l'Orient de Marseille, entre 1762 et 1787 (Brussels: Ed. Memo & Codec, 1986), 47 and 49.

18 *Tableau des Frères qui composent la T.R. Loge Saint Jean d'Ecosse, à l'Orient de Marseille [...] 1784* ("List of the Brothers in the *Saint Jean d'Ecosse* Lodge, in the Orient of Marseille [...] 1784,") [printed], Lib. GODF AR 113-2, item 517.

19 Rite Primitif, *Tableau de la première [loge] du Rite Primitif en France* (Narbonne, 1790).

20 From the first half of the eighteenth century, it was common to see a rapprochement between Freemasonry and the knightly orders, and many Lodges used the name *Saint John of Jerusalem*. The Lodge created in Nancy in 1772 still exists today, under the Obedience of the Grand Orient de France.

21 Alain Blondy, *L'Ordre de Malte au XVIIIᵉ siècle*, 267.

22 Strasbourg National University Library, Manuscript 5437, *Registre des procès-verbaux de la loge de la Candeur constituée mère des loges du Grand Orient de Strasbourg*, f° 176. Our thanks to Pierre-Yves Beaurepaire for bringing this reference to our attention.

23 Pierre-Yves Beaurepaire, *L'autre et le Frère, l'étranger et la Franc-maçonnerie*

When *Saint John's Lodge of Secrecy and Harmony* reformed in 1788, it showed great concern to establish solid relationships with England. The correspondence contains many expressions of allegiance to the Grand Lodge of London. The Brothers emphasize "*the Most Reverend Brother the Count von Kolowrat [... who made us] determined to resume our works under the regime of the Supreme Lodge of England.*" He was the man in charge of presenting and defending the case before the English, with whom he seemed to have privileged links.[24] However, Kolowrat was not only the guarantor of the London-Malta link. He also maintained strong relationships with other European Masonic centers. Thus, a few years before, he took part in an important event for French and German Masonries. It is surprising to find on the "*Table of deputies in the General Congress of Freemasons under the Rectified Rite gathered in Wilhelmsbad from July 16 to September 1, 1782 [...] the Count von Kolowrat Liebstein, Chamberlain to H.M. Imperial, in O. Fr. Franciscus Eq. Ab Aquila fulgente, with the full powers of the Chapter of Saint Hypolite in Vienna and of Hermandstadt in Transylvania.*"[25] Introduced into the Grand Lodge of England, Brother Kollowrat was also a familiar of Germanic Masonry. However, the international contacts of the Maltese Lodge also extended to other areas. At a time when the Brothers were trying to establish themselves under English protection, some of the most eminent members of the Lodge being composed also belonged to another Lodge in Rome, this time under the Paris Obedience. In fact, a record of the *Réunion des Amis Intimes* is to be found in the archives of the Grand Orient de France,[26] for which the

---

en France au XVIIIe siècle France (Paris: Honoré Champion, 1998), particularly Chapter 9: "La Candeur, orient de Strasbourg: un creuset maçonnique," 399–443. At the start of the 1770s, there was another Maltese knight in the ranks: de Brühl.

24 In fact, the register of the Grand Secretary of London includes several letters exchanged with Kolowrat, particularly on the affairs of Naples where Masonry had been banned. These show a mutual understanding between the two correspondents. See Alain Blondy, *L'Ordre de Malte au XVIIIe siècle*, 76.

25 Grand Prieuré des Gaules, Les Cahiers verts, *Les Convents du Régime Ecossais Rectifié*, special edition (Paris, 2005), 144–146.

26 The Grand Orient de France's correspondence archives for this period are cur-

Master in 1789 was the bailiff Abel de Loras. Its members included Count von Kolowrat and the knight Guillet de Monthoux, Loras's nephew and adoptive son.

This situation illustrates both the mobility of Malta's high executives within Enlightenment Europe and the way in which the new Masonic network was coupled with and completed the old Maltese network. In the late 1780s, the (main?) Lodge of Malta, which seems to have been a sort of annex of a part of the Order's leadership, was consequently in contact with the Masonic centers of London, Paris, and Rome, with a few connections in Germany and Austria. Again, over-interpretation should be avoided. However, it is necessary to note that in Malta, Loras and Kolowrat were the leaders of the party wishing to free the Order from the direct and predominant influence of Versailles. The Grand Master had even stopped making decisions of any importance without the approval of the French Ministry. The enemies of the "French party" wanted to give the Order back some room for maneuver by rebalancing the powers that influenced it, particularly by trying to preserve relationships with the Court of Naples, with Spain in the background, and by bringing new players like Russia or England onto the Mediterranean scene. Thus, it is highly likely that the attachment of the *Secrecy and Harmony* to London, on Kolowrat's initiative, was not purely driven by Masonic motives. However, the affair would end badly. Loras[27] was in Rome in 1789, responsible for representing the Order to the Pope. He wanted to be made an official ambassador for Malta. Obviously, being both a representative of the Sovereign Order of Saint John of Jerusalem to the Holy See and a Worshipful Master chairing over a Lodge of the Grand Orient could pose

---

rently kept in the *Cabinet des manuscrits*. BnF, FM² 575.

27 Loras has a bad reputation and historians are often very critical about him. Without wishing to plead in his defense, two points explaining this severity can be discussed. Firstly, he was one of the main players of the party which was in fact hostile to France, which obviously wins him no favor from a primarily French historiography. Secondly, most of the accounts about his personality are from his sworn enemy (who was nevertheless a Brother in knighthood and Masonry), Dolomieu.

problems for fault-finders.[28] However, his links with Cagliostro also worked against him. High on the list of the Inquisition's investigation of the "Grand Copht" of "Egyptian Masonry," he was forced to flee by night to Naples, where he took refuge. He then moved on to Malta, where (with mixed success) he tried to return to grace with the Grand Master Rohan.

Three Good Reasons for Knights to be Masons

The cosmopolitanism to which knights were in some ways predisposed was one of the factors explaining their relative enthusiasm for Freemasonry, but it was not the only reason. There was also the spirit of the times, and Alain Blondy rightly emphasizes that it was in no way unusual for a knight of Malta in the eighteenth century to be a Mason. Knights were simply like the young, well-off people of any period, who had the leisure to take an interest in the innovations of their time. They could not remain unaware of the papal condemnation, but it is clear that few of them were frightened by it. Speaking to his ambassador in Rome, Cardinal Fleury answered without illusion that: *"The bull that the Pope has issued against the Freemasons may not be enough to abolish this Brotherhood, if there is no penalty besides the fear of excommunication. The court of Rome applies this penalty so often that today, it has little preventive power."*[29]

Aside from the spirit of the times (Marie-Antoinette wrote to her sister that *"everyone is a Freemason"*[30]) there are two more unexpected factors that explain the Masonic commitment of the knights of Malta. The first also concerns the mentality of the time, although in another register. Certain high-society Lodges were simply centers for noble sociability in the eighteenth century. Thus, the *Société Olympique* emanating from the *Olympique de la Parfaite Es-*

---

28 The person finally named as ambassador, Camille de Rohan, also occupied these two positions.

29 Translated from Pierre Chevallier, *Le Sceptre, la Crosse et l'Equerre sous Louis XV et Louis XVI 1725–1789* (Paris: Honoré Champion, 1996), 76.

30 Translation of Pierre Chevallier's citation in: *Histoire de la Franc-maçonnerie française* (Paris: Fayard, 1974), t.I, 209. Source: Paul Vogt d'Hunolstein, *Correspondance inédite de Marie-Antoinette* (Paris: Dentu, 1864).

time Lodge contained 9 princes, 13 dukes, 55 marquises, 57 counts, 19 viscounts, and 13 barons... including 17 Knights of Malta, one of whom was the great Suffren. The *Candeur* Lodge (closely linked to Orléans) and the *Contrat Social* Lodge also contained many Maltese Masons. Similar situations were seen in the provinces although to a lesser extent. For example, in Toulouse, although there were several Knights of Malta in the ranks of the *Vérité Reconnue* Lodge, this was primarily because it was a meeting point for the local aristocracy. In fact, it was *"by far the most exclusive Lodge in the town, because it contained not only magistrates, military personnel, and gentlemen, but also no commoners, and because there were clearly more nobles of the sword than nobles of the robe."*[31]

A third and final, more subtle and even more mysterious motive further explains the presence of knights in Lodges: some showed a clear interest in Christian esotericism. We will not retrace the relations between Loras and Cagliostro here. However, it is also unusual to observe the relative over-representation of the Maltese in Lodges professing the Rectified Scottish Rite: Chefdebien in Narbonne, Aigrefeuille in Montpellier then in Paris, du Bourg and Guibert in Toulouse, La Croix de Sayve in Grenoble, Monspey in Lyon . . . As for Kolowrat, he participated, but Chefdebien was also there at the founding event of the Rite: the Congress of Wilhelmsbad. Yet the Rectified Scottish Rite and its Order of Benevolent Knights of the Holy City saw themselves as restoring true chivalry in service of the most essential mysteries of Christianity. Its structures were those of an Order of chivalry. Its ceremonies and its instructions were meant to explain the relationships between God, men, and the universe by the mediation of Jesus Christ and intermediary spirits. The Knights of Malta therefore practiced a very distinctive type of Masonry.

The work of the Congress of Wilhelmsbad provides an interesting account of the esoteric speculations of certain Knights of Malta at debates concerning whether the Templars held occult knowledge.

---

31 Translated from Michel Taillefer, *La Franc-maçonnerie Toulousaine: 1741– 1799* (Paris: Commission d'Histoire de la Révolution Française/ENSB-CTHS, 1984), 133.

Brother Willermoz made a parallel with the Order of Malta and evoked the case of knights versed in these issues. The issue discussed was the presence, in the very structure of the Order of the Temple, of elements linked to the numerical symbolism that is so important in Freemasonry in general, and in the professed gnosis of theosophist Masons in particular:

We can observe that at the time of its greatest splendor, it was divided into nine Provinces, each governed by a Provincial Leader, that the number of nine leaders corresponds to the number of founders, coming to ten with its General Grand Master. Some state that this number expresses great things: this observation, which is rather indifferent to me, might be scorned and mocked by some, and perhaps it will also retain the attention of others. As for me, I leave it to each individual according to the meaning they wish to give it, noting only that when we want to verify the origin and goal of an Order or Society, we must not neglect any of the keys that might help with this verification. I further observe that the Order of Malta, born in the same place in almost the same period, appears to have been established on the same basis that it still retains today, although some tongues of this Order have ceased their action. Even today, it is represented in Malta by nine pillars or Order leaders under different names, who with their Grand Master make ten, and, in the General Chapters, by 27 representatives, who with the same Grand Master make 28, which comes down to the same; this conformity is interesting, and perhaps we might manage to find some even more interesting causes for it in the old archives of the Order. I know several of its members who are convinced of this.[32]

---

32 Translated from: Grand Prieuré des Gaules, Les Cahiers verts, "Préavis du Fr. ab Eremo, Gr. Grand Prieuré des Gaules, Les Cahiers verts,Chancelier de la IIᵉ [province ...] sur la question concernant la légitimité de la filiation de l'O. du T. avec notre système actuel [...]," *Les Convents du Régime Ecossais Rectifié*, special edition, 53–54.

These interesting words were spoken at a small gathering before at least two other Knights of Malta: the Brothers (in Masonry) *Eques a Capite Galeato* (Chefdebien) and *ab Aquila Fulgente* (Kolowrat). Silence equals consent! The Maltese were perhaps also looking for an ideal (fantasy) chivalry in the High Degrees of Masonry: one which they could not find in the everyday life of the Order.[33]

Whatever the private reasons (social or "esoteric") which brought them to the Lodge, the knights subsequently practiced Masonry across Europe. Whether their works were in the spirit of Diderot's Encyclopedia or whether they heralded a romantic quest, for the Knights of Malta, membership of a Lodge was above all a way of being in their century, a means of connection to the present of their time. However, by partaking in this new sociability, which was the more or less legitimate offspring of Enlightenment thinkers, they in fact participated in a great change in minds and in a revolution "which everything seemed to portend, yet which nobody saw coming,"[34] according to the pertinent observation of Brother de Ségur.

It is necessary to avoid any anachronism. Although many eighteenth-century Lodges were sensitive to new ideas, they cannot under any circumstances be considered as a whole to have been a militant wing of the *philosophical party*. The fact that many Knights of Malta were Masons should not be interpreted as a conversion of Voltaire's and Diderot's ideas. One current of Masonry, well-represented in Malta, arises more from a pre-romantic sensibility, or even from what could be called the "anti-Enlightenment thinkers." Masonic initiation was in this case probably experienced as a way of reconnecting with the true knightly essence of the Order. From the 1790s, the strong presence of Masonry at the highest level of Saint John of Jerusalem provoked comments about a "Masonic con-

---

33 Pierre Mollier, *La Chevalerie maçonnique: imaginaire chevaleresque, légende templière et Franc-maçonnerie au siècle des Lumières* (Paris: Dervy, 2005).

34 *Mémoires du Comte de Ségur*, Tome II, 95. The Count of Ségur was not Maltese, but he left an excellent description of his reception into the *Ordre de Saint Lazare*, comparing this venerable ceremony and the evolution of the century.

spiracy" which supposedly influenced the leaders of the Order and finally led to the fall of Malta. This theory attributes to it a unity of thought and action that it never possessed and still does not possess. Thus, two of the most significant Mason-Knights, Loras and Dolomieu, fought so bitterly that if Masonry did in a way weaken the Order, it was more by internal disputes than by any mythical conspiracy! However, the Maltese Lodge, with its branches in the main European capitals, brought together knights who defended fairly similar positions within Saint John of Jerusalem. Consequently, it seems that Masonry did constitute a sort of "party" with Loras and Kolowrat as its figureheads. This party had a following in de Rohan's Princedom and attempted to play a part after 1797. For a while, in fact, *the bailiff de Loras, having subjugated the Grand Master, controlled [...] the policy of Malta.*[35] Thus the "Lodge of the knights" probably had an influence, but its real nature and extent are difficult to judge in the power balances among which Malta tried to defend its position in the Mediterranean setting.

---

35 Translated from Alain Blondy, *L'Ordre de Malte au XVIIIᵉ siècle*, 258–259.

The Stuarts and Freemasonry: The Final Episode

The connection between the Stuarts and Freemasonry remains one of the key elements in the Masonic imagination of the eighteenth century. Many rituals or correspondence documents explain that since time immemorial, the Stuarts were the protectors and secret leaders of the Order. Some even add that the Lodges had a hidden goal to reinstate the unfortunate Scottish dynasty to their legitimate place on the throne. Perhaps there is no smoke without fire, but historians today can still find no documented testimonies on the real involvement of the "pretenders" into Freemasonry. Rare elements emerge, such as the attested existence of a "Jacobite" Lodge in Rome in James III of England's entourage, or that of a few Stuartist Lodges identified in Paris in the 1730s by Pierre Chevallier. However, conversely, all the patents or charters supposedly granted, signed, or promulgated by the Stuarts have proven to be false. Before looking deeper into the matter, it is useful to retrace the history of the legend.

From 1653, the Perth Lodge exhibited a parchment asserting that James VI of Scotland was received as an Entered Apprentice on April 15, 1601. From 1737, there were rumors among Parisian Masons about the existence of a Lodge during the exile (from 1688) in Saint-Germain-en-Laye. In 1749, the ritual of the Sublime Order of Knights Elect asserted that the pursued Templars were welcomed and protected by the Stuart Kings in Scotland, where they hid in Masonic Lodges. The legend thrived even more thanks to the strong romantic dimension it gained from the personality, saga, and tragic fate of Bonnie Prince Charlie—Charles Edward Stuart, known as the "young pretender" (1720–1788). I would like to take this opportunity to relate a later but very real episode, in which the last Stuart became involved in Freemasonry[1] to (finally!) take on the role of secret Grand Master that everyone credited him with.

1777: "Successor to My Ancestors in Masonry"

Probably from the 1740s, and certainly in 1749, the Sublime Order of Knights Elect asserted that modern Freemasonry came from the Templars who escaped persecution at the hands of Philippe le Bel (Philip IV of France) and took refuge in Scotland under the protection of the Stuart Kings. The three ingredients of this "Templar legend" (the Order of the Temple, Scotland, and the Stuarts) are seen in many of the Chivalric High Degrees, which expanded from 1750. Given the dynamism of the Lodges in the eighteenth century, including in the high aristocracy of the European courts, the question of their real connections with Freemasonry was necessarily asked of the Stuarts themselves by some of their eminent interlocutors. In his meeting with Baron de Waechter, Charles Edward confirmed that he discussed Freemasonry with his father "on several occasions."

Whether calculatingly (as in the accusations of modern critics) or in good faith as I believe, Baron von Hund, "Eques ab Ense i.o.," preserved this Templar and Stuartist genealogy when he began developing the "Templar Strict Observance" in Germany from 1750. He claimed that he had been received in Paris in the 1740s, into the restored Order of the Temple, within a Lodge bringing together English and Scottish members of the entourage of Charles Edward Stuart, the "young pretender." He was led to believe that Charles Edward was the secret Grand Master of the Masons, under the name "Eques a Sole Aureo." The Freemasonry that concealed the secret continuation of the Order of the Temple was in reality led

---

1   My attention was brought to this matter by a note from my friend Pierre Noël in "Réaction à la conférence 'Un rituel inédit de langue française, daté de 1758,'" *Acta Macionica* 11 (2001): 359–360. Noël refers to the published work that contains some of the documents relating to Charles Edward's declarations on Freemasonry during his exile in Florence: Pericle Maruzzi, *La Stretta Osservanza Templare e il Regime Scozzese Rettificato in Italia nel secolo XVIII* (Rome: Atanòr, 1990).

by "Unknown Superiors." He was finally entrusted with the restoration of the "Seventh Province," between the Elbe and the Oder, of the Order of the Temple. From 1770, the Order became increasingly successful. However, at the same time, its founder gradually lost his influence, while that of dignitaries of a higher social rank increased. Thus, after his death on October 28, 1776, the leadership of the Order fell into the hands of two rival princes: Ferdinand, Duke of Brunswick-Lüneburg, "Eques a Victoria i.o.," and Charles, Duke of Sudermania, "Eques a Sole Vivificante i.o." and brother of King Gustav III of Sweden, himself "Eques a Corona Vindicata i.o." They were significant figures in Europe during the 1770s and 1780s, which helps to explain the three events that I am about to recount.

The nagging question of the origins of the Order and the somewhat muddled explanations from its founder, Baron von Hund, perturbed and divided several Convents of the Strict Observance. In 1777, shortly after becoming Magnus Magister Ordinis, Ferdinand of Brunswick sent a very active Mason, Baron de Waechter—Eques a Ceraso—to the "young pretender," (who in fact was no longer young), to (finally!) interrogate him "officially" on the real connections between the Stuarts and Freemasonry.

That Charles Edward[2] participated with good grace was clearly owing to the eminent rank of the duke who sent Waechter, but also undoubtedly because he was in a very difficult situation at the time. The days when Europe was passionate about the Stuartist cause—when they had great support from continental monarchies, and when the exploits of 1745 were fresh in everyone's minds—had long passed. In that year, Bonnie Prince Charlie (who was barely twenty-five years old) had arrived in Scotland and narrowly missed regaining his throne with the support of his Highlanders. This saga had kept the whole of Europe on the edge of its seat. Thirty years on, everyone had long stopped believing that the Stuarts would return,

---

2   On the life of Charles Edward Stuart, it is useful to consult Michel Duchein's *Les derniers Stuarts 1660–1807* (Paris: Fayard, 2006), particularly Chapter 13, "La Fin des Stuarts 1744–1807," on the end of the Stuarts. Also useful is the reference biography published by Frank McLynn, *Charles Edward Stuart: A Tragedy in Many Acts* (London: Routledge, 1988).

and the major states had finally normalized their relations with Hanoverian England. At fifty-seven years old, Charles Edward was a man broken by political and personal failures and diminished by alcohol. It was all he could do to welcome the eminent people who took an interest in him, even if they did so for unusual reasons.

Waechter was a lawyer, and he left a precise account of his meeting with Charles Edward, who at the time was hiding (without really fooling anyone) behind the title of the Count of Albany. The text[3] is fascinating, and I would like to offer readers a full reproduction of this very lively account:

> *The Privy Counsellor of Waechter's Legation for the Duke of Saxe-Gotha, having been a deputy in the united lodges of Germany and of the Neighboring States, asked the Count of Albany whether he had been told by his late Father that the Dignity of Grand Master of the Freemasons had been hereditary in the illustrious House of the Stuarts since King Charles II of Great Britain, whether he had consequently received the related Papers & Documents, whether he wished to transmit them to the united Lodges, thereby legitimating himself as the Grand Master & Leader, & being recognized by those in this eminent Charge to their reciprocal benefits;*

> *The said Privy Counsellor of Waechter's Legations requested that the Count tell him the day & time when he might have the honor of discussing with him the important subject of his Commission; the Count did this, giving him this day, and he discharged his Commission by informing the Count of the intentions of the united Lodges, & requesting that he answer honestly, as could be expected of a man of universally recognized probity, & trusting his honor concerning the absolute silence that the importance of the affair required from both Parties.*

---

3   Transcribed and published in Maruzzi, *La Stretta Osservanza Templare*, 96–98.

*The Count was kind enough to answer this proposal by say-
ing that he had not been informed at all of anything that
might be connected with Masonry, that, given that several
illustrious men of his House had been Masons, he had several times indicated to his late Father his desire to become
one, but that his father had always opposed this; that his
late father had told him several times that he was not a Mason, that he had therefore not given to him any Paper on
the matter, and that if he had been so himself, his extreme
devotion would certainly have led him to renounce Masonry after the late Pope Benedict XIV's Bull condemning it;
that he possessed many Papers belonging to his late Father
and kept in Rome, but that he was sure they could contain
nothing of interest, because his brother had assured him of
this, after examining them.*

*That his late father had left him two more Crates full of
Papers, but that these were sealed in St. Germain en Laye,
& that he had so far not expected any certain chance to send
for them, although he believed that the crate he had not yet
opened contained nothing relating to Masonry. He declared
his intention to do this immediately, & stated that he was
consequently very disposed to contribute in any way to the
Objectives that the united Lodges might have, but he was
only obliged to declare in advance that he could spend nothing in this whole affair, & to beg that the Privy Counsellor
of Waechter's Legation agree a Figure with him to recipro-
cally communicate useful News.*

*The Count answered two other questions from the Privy
Counsellor of Waechter's Legation: whether a certain Lord
Sackville had been connected to his late Father & whether
the Count had had in his service, several years ago, a certain
Giacomo Approsi? That he had never known the former,
that Lord Guérit had been his last secretary, & that he had
not been in his service for three years, and that he took take
of his affairs himself.*

The Privy Counsellor of Waechter's Legation then asked the Count to give him permission to produce an Extract of their Interview, to make two copies of it, & to leave one with the Count, & use the other to give himself legitimacy with the Masonic Superiors, the Count gave his permission readily, also making a solemn promise to maintain perfect silence about [this] whole affair, & upon receiving that of the said Privy Counsellor of Waechter's Legation, to only give Report of it to the Masonic Superiors.

The Count, in witness of the above, put his seal on a Copy & received from the Privy Counsellor of Waechter's Legation another, also signed and sealed with his mark.

Written in Florence, September 21 of the Year 1777.

Note.

All of this was written in the Count of Albany's own hand:

Nothing in the world could flatter me more & I would consider it a very great honor if I were to be recognized as successor to my ancestors in Masonry

Florence, September 21, 1777

[signed] *Count of Albany*

Charles Edward's answers were sincere, but of course deceptive for adepts of the Templar and Jacobite origins of Masonry. However, the last phrase left a mixed impression, and these due confessions would not definitively close the debate. By attributing the origins and leadership of the Order to "Unknown Superiors" whose mystery masked the significance, Baron von Hund had, undoubtedly involuntarily, invented a formidable concept. Charles Edward's denials and his uncomfortable response do not in any way prove he was not the Unknown Superior. After all, by definition, did such superiors not have to do everything they could to conceal their status and mission? Moreover, as a repercussion of the failure of 1745 and his shady and unpredictable character, from 1750 and until his father died in 1766, Charles Edward led a rather mysterious life: for no real reason, he disappeared. He became anonymous: hidden behind various pseudonyms and an unremarkable appearance, he traveled Europe unbeknown to everyone, even those closest to him. Nobody knew where he was. Of course, from time to time, he was recognized, but a few days later, he would disappear again and nobody would hear of him for months, until a police force traced him in another town. It was an astonishing way of life, which in combination with his well-known taste for secrecy and dissimulation[4] made the idea of an "Unknown Superior" on a secret mission credible. Still, contact was maintained. Waechter wrote to him regularly to obtain information on various details of the history of the Stuarts and their partisans that might potentially reveal connections with Freemasonry.[5] German Masons also showed great interest in the papers of James II kept in Saint-Germain-en-Laye, but Charles Edward ignored them. Waechter even sent an emissary to Florence to try and get them. He was turned away, and when Waechter was surprised by this, Charles Edward answered that since the emissary had not introduced himself as a representative of the Masons, he had feared it was a trap!

1780: The First Swedish Attempt

Under the direction of Baron von Hund, the "Seventh Province" of the Strict Templar Observance had been the cradle for the modern renaissance of the Order. Hund's disappearance in 1776 marked the start of a period of intense negotiations for the succession of Eques ab Ense. After three years, in spite of major reservations on the part of Ferdinand of Brunswick, who was hardly pleased to see an important figure counteracting his authority at the head of the Order, the Duke of Sudermania was finally named Grand Master of the

---

4   As emphasized by his biographer Frank McLynn in *Charles Edward Stuart*, 533.

5   Elements reported by Frank McLynn based on the "Stuart Papers" kept at Windsor, in McLynn, *Charles Edward Stuart*, 534.

Seventh Province. Whether he was not familiar with the "Waechter Report," or whether he did not believe it, several weeks after beginning his new functions, on December 11, 1779, he decided to inform Charles Edward. It is true that in Stockholm, the Master of Ceremonies of the Court, Brother von Plommenfeldt, was a firm believer in the Jacobite affiliation and claimed to have received proof of it from Charles Edward himself during a trip to Florence. On January 18, 1780, Duke Charles wrote the following letter to the "pretender."[6]

> *The first duty of every man of honor is to try and be able, with the Help of the very high, to meet the Commitments he has made, & to try in his behavior to merit the Esteem of those who Are above him & the Trust of those who must obey him, I am currently performing one of these duties, & performing it with even greater Pleasure because in doing so, I hope to be able to establish a close Liaison with a Prince famous for both his Virtues and his misfortunes, whom I have always held in infinite esteem. Having been elected Leader of the Seventh Province, it is my duty to pay the tribute I owe to my Leader to the Grand Master of our Holy Order. By the sublime Theoretical Wisdom entrusted to me by Brother von Plommenfeldt in the Knightly Order known as Stella immaculata & in the Sanctuary known under the Name of Bias, which he brought from Florence, I learned to know my Grand Master & the Grand Master of the whole Holy Order, who I had long desired to know; but let him not himself refuse me the Certainty I have just received from his Person, & let him be Good enough to ratify with an Act of his hand, the Choice that the Seventh Province has just made. The Laws that have been entrusted to me order that all the Leaders of Provinces must be named or approved by the Grand Master, & I am the first to desire that this Law be applied to me.*

---

6   Working documents of the Convent of Wilhelmsbad, Library of the Grand Orient de France, donated by Alain Bauer, AR.

Very enlightened, very Illustrious, & very worthy Brother, if you grant me Your suffrage, allow me to report to you the detail of the Province & give me Your orders by Consequence, I will look upon You as a Father, consider myself a son who, enlightened by Your Advice, will take double pleasure in fulfilling Commitments made out of pure Zeal for the Holy Order at the Feet of its altars & of which the sincere objective is to persevere to the detriment of all else, to reach A close liaison with these tender Fathers who made a spark of the true Light shine in out Northern Climates. Convinced that my pleas will not be refused & that You will not turn away a Child who has so long sought his Father without success, & who hopes in finding him to find within himself the aim & the recompense for all the works. If I am permitted this hope, my Gratitude will be eternal & will increase my strength so that I can acquire the Qualities to deserve the Trust that I dare to request. But if my Wishes are not heeded, I will content myself in my Grief with the little that I know, I will arm myself with the Patience of Job, & I will await with Resignation the right moment when he Wishes to look upon me. I will however have fulfilled my duty, & I will inside myself restrict myself to making the ardent Vows I must make to earn the Trust of my Superior & of my Leader. It is with these sentiments that I recommend myself, very enlightened, very Illustrious, & very worthy Brother in Your tender friendship, with the highest Respect, & inviolable Affection.

Very enlightened, very Illustrious, & very worthy Brother,
Stockholm, January 18, 1780.
Your affectionate & devoted Brother
Carolus a Sole vivificante Dux Sud

To this eloquent and lengthy missive, the "Count of Albany" gave a very cordial reply—though one that was also belated, short, and rather disappointing:

My eternal affection and gratitude for the very obliging Let-
ter that H.R.H. kindly wrote to me through Mr. Borguin-
stierna. The New Degree that he has just received could not
have fallen into better Hands.

The total Darkness in which I reside concerning the Mys-
teries prevents me from saying anything further, until I am
Enlightened. I beg HRH to be persuaded of my respect &
the sincere affection I will always have for Him and his au-
gust Family.

The C. of Al. Sept 25, 1780.

But once again, this admission of ignorance from the pretender, as clear as it may be, only convinced those who wanted to be
convinced. Was his awkwardness in itself not suspicious? The formidable notion of the Unknown Superior once more provided an
explanation for these uncomfortable denials: the duty of secrecy. It
is worth noting that the Duke of Sudermania did envisage this hypothesis at the end of his letter, in which he announces his patient
resignation if his request is not granted.

1783: An Authentic Jacobite Masonic Patent

The Swedish, fervent believers in the Jacobite filiation, made a third
attempt. This would be a success. It is possible that the apparent
credulity of the Stockholm dignitaries also hid various political
agendas. An authentic document from the Stuart pretender was
a major advantage with regard to Masonic figures in their rivalry
with Ferdinand von Brunswick. Moreover, Gustav III had in mind
a claim to Livonia, which in the Middle Ages was under the rule of
the Teutonic Order. A title on the Order of the Temple—assimilat-
ed on this occasion with the Teutonics—could provide an additional argument. The fact remains that, during a visit to Italy, the King
of Sweden made the pilgrimage to Florence. In December 1783,[7]

---

7   There is some doubt concerning the exact date of the meeting. Claude Nord-
    mann (see below) uses the Swedish royal archives to date it to December 21,

Gustav III accompanied by his friend and favorite Armfelt, whose father had participated in the Forty-Five, visited Charles Edward and had several discussions with him.[8] He was profoundly moved by the distress of James II's grandson,[9] who was aging, abandoned by his young wife, penniless, and without support. The "young pretender," now a slightly senile old man who struggled to walk, told him the same anecdotes several times. The King of Sweden wrote to Louis XVI and to the King of Spain to obtain assistance for him, and also granted him an annual pension of five hundred pounds from his personal treasury. Shortly afterwards, in Rome, he arranged with the Holy See under the best conditions his separation from the Countess of Albany. It was at this time that, out of gratitude, Charles Edward granted the title he so desired. But beyond the different services that he received from Gustav III, Charles Edward was above all struck by the fact that the King of a European power, for the first time in so long, had come to see him ex officio, and treated him respectfully, as an equal. This was in contrast to the Grand Duke of Tuscany, who in ten years had not deigned to travel five hundred meters to come and see him.

Thus, for the first time, the only authentic Jacobite Masonic patent is revealed:

We Charles Edward[10]

1783, but the patent signed by Charles Edward (of which we only possess a copy and not the original, possibly incorrect on this matter: 8 for 28?) is dated December 8.

8 René Leforestier, *La Franc-Maçonnerie Occultiste et Templière aux XVIIIe et XIXe siècles*, 2 vols. (Paris: La Table d'Emeraude, 1987); this second edition published by Antoine Faivre includes addenda and an index. The author briefly relates the episode in a note (2:698n54). He indicates that the English diplomatic archives retain traces of these meetings in the reports sent to London by Sir Horace Mann, British ambassador in Florence, whose informer, it seems, was the same Chevalier des Tours who organized the meeting.

9 These elements are taken from: Claude Nordmann, *Gustave III, un démocrate couronné* (Lille: Presses Universitaires de Lille, 1986), 219.

10 Facsimile of the French copy of the patent, private collection. My warmest thanks go to my dear Brother and friend S. for having made this extremely rare document available to me.

*By the grace of God Sovereign Leader and Hereditary Grand
Master of the Holy Order of the Knights of Saint John of the
Temple of our Lord Jesus Christ, last Prince and legitimate
Heir of the Royal House of the Stuarts, to all our dear and
respectable brothers who will read these patent letters, Salu-
tations.*

*Considering that we have no children, that the life of man
is in the hands of God, his eternal wisdom can prolong it for
more long years as well as cutting it short and ending it when
we least expect it, and that by the laws of this Holy Order,
of which the Supreme Government and the hereditary Grand
Mastery have been passed down to us by the Kings our Ancestors and our Predecessors, we are obliged not to let this
Eminent Dignity die out in our person, who as the last of the
Royal House of the Stuarts possesses it; we have taken it upon
ourselves to choose and elect a Successor and a Coadjutor in
hereditary Grand Mastery of the Order, who after our death
can succeed us in governing it, which following this choice must
always remain under the direction of a supreme Leader, who
can at the same time protect it and maintain its laws in their
purity.*

*Then considering that this Dignity must always be exercised
by a crowned head, as it was conferred by the unanimous votes
of the whole Order to the first King of our House who held it
and from whom we have received it, we have not only found
in the zeal for the Order and in the virtues that have long
shone out in the actions of the Very High, very powerful, and
very Excellent Prince GUSTAV III by the grace of God King
of Sweden, of the Goths, and the Vandals, Heir of Norway,
Duke of Schleswig-Holstein, Stormarn and Ditmarsh, Count
of Oldenburg and of Delmenhorst, in Ordine Dicts: Equite de
Corona Vindicata, all the qualities that we might wish for the
good of the Order, but also that this Prince, whose House has
for several centuries often been allied with ours, has been the
only one of our family who has shown interest in our misfor-*

tune. Wishing therefore to show him our gratitude, this considered, we have declared, as we presently declare, that should we have the misfortune to leave behind us no legitimate male child, we have named, elected, and chosen the aforementioned GUSTAV III King of the Goths and Vandals as our Coadjutor and Successor in the hereditary Grand Mastery of the Holy Order of the Temple of Our Lord Jesus Christ, He and his male Successors to the Royal throne of Sweden, born to a legitimate marriage and admitted as Freemasons according to the laws of the Order, with all the rights, prerogatives, immunities, and power with which we and our predecessors have exercised this Dignity.

We order all those who are under our obedience, Provinces, their leaders, Directories, Grand Priors and other officers, Chapters and all the Knightly Brothers of the said Order, to recognize by virtue of these irrevocable patent letters the aforementioned Very High, Very Powerful, And Very Excellent Prince GUSTAV III, by the grace of God King of Sweden and of the Goths and Vandals, Heir of Norway, Duke of Schleswig-Holstein, Stormarn, and Ditmarsh, Count of Oldenburg and of Delmenhorst, in Ordine Dictum: Equitem de Corona Vindicata, as our Coadjutor in the Grand Mastery and after Our death as Sovereign Leader and hereditary Grand Master of the Order, and to obey him in this role, as the laws of the Order require.

By naming this Prince as our Successor, we fulfill the duty that our affection for the Order /demands of us and confirm this election, which we wish to be seen as our supreme, final, and irrevocable/ will on the sacred numbers of Three, Four, and Nine.

In witness whereof, we have signed the present papers in our hand and marked them with our seal

Signed in Florence, this December 8, MDCCLXXXIII

(□)
S[ign]*ed* \ *[Masonic characters]* +
Charles

S[ign]*ed*\ *knight*
CMistowy
Genal Secretary +"

However, a witness[11] asserts that Gustav III was (justifiably!) disappointed not to find in his interlocutor the esoteric wisdom that Plommenfeldt had praised so highly. Perhaps he put it down to Charles Edward's age and to the illness that had weakened him so greatly.

Even though (or perhaps because) all of this was secret, the news traveled fast. In a letter to the Brothers of Strasbourg, Doctor Giraud, one of the Italian dignitaries of the Order, wrote on February 21, 1784, barely three months after the precious document was awarded:

> *I bring you strange news that will make you laugh! Before the death of the Pretender [?] the King of Sweden went to see him, had several conferences with him, & finally asked him in exchange for the sum of a Thousand louis d'or for the resignation of his place of Grand Master of the Order of the T . . . , which the pretender resigned very willingly as you would imagine; & consequently he gave him a Patent, which Sweden will invoke.[12]*

It was perhaps "news that will make you laugh" because everyone in Italy knew of Charles Edward's pitiful state. However, it is also possible that the laughter of Giraud and the Alsatian brothers was forced. Partisans of Ferdinand von Brunswick, they were fully aware of the advantage that the precious parchment gave his competitors. Learning of Gustav III's nomination as coadjutor, Waechter rushed

---

11 The Chevalier des Tours, who organized the meeting, cited by René Leforestier in *La Franc-Maçonnerie Occultiste et Templière*, 698n54.

12 Transcribed and published in Maruzzi, *La Stretta Osservanza Templare*, 99.

to Florence, counting on his good relationship with Charles Edward to defend the rights of Ferdinand von Brunswick. However, he did not arrive until April 1784, three months after Gustav's departure with his real Jacobite patent in hand![13] In the margin of the original of Giraud's letter, Brother de Turckeim has written:

Meiningen, May 15, 1784.[14]

According to news from Rome, found in Gotha, the King of Sweden has not only bought the proclaimed or imaginary rights of the Stuart Prince to the General Grand Mastery of the Order, but the King himself has become a Roman Catholic, & had the Pope rehabilitate the Ancient O. of the T., of which the officers of the King's entourage openly wear, it is said, the little red cross on their clothes & therefore the entourage is once again bringing the Cross into the Grand Order of Sweden known as the Seraphs.

The Swedish were quick to report their new title. The archives of the Province of Burgundy kept a copy of the following account:

The Grand Master of the Holy Order of the Knights of Saint John of the Temple of our Lord Jesus Christ names for his coadjutor G. A. [that is, Gustave Adolphe] in Ord. dictus Eques a Corona vindicata, by a patent that he sent to him when he was at his home in Florence on December 8, 1783.[15]

This patent is signed Brother Charles ✠.

The patent was read in the Chapter of the Masters of the Temple in S.[Stockholm] on March 22, 1785, and the record of this reading is signed Nicolaus Bielke ✠.

---

13 Elements reported by Frank McLynn based on the "Stuart Papers" kept at Windsor, in McLynn, *Charles Edward Stuart*, 535.

14 Transcribed and published in Maruzzi, *La Stretta Osservanza Templare*, 100.

15 Transcribed and published in Maruzzi, *La Stretta Osservanza Templare*, 100.

On the death of C: E: [Charles Edward Stuart] *this piece was once again exhibited & approved, & placed on the protocol of the Chapter of the M*[asters of the] *T*[emple] *on April 18, 1788.*

Written on it are the words:

Defuncto C. E. in Capitulo M. T. die 18 aprilis 1788 denuo exibitum & approbatum ut in protocollo.

Nicolaus Cornes Bielke +

M.C. IX.^{ae} Prov.^{ae}

Eques a Sole aureo succedit 1743. Moritur 31. Januar. 1788.

G... in ordine dictus Eques et Frater professus a Corona vindicata succedit 31. Januar. 1788. Agnoscitur a + [i. e. Capitulo] *Can*[onicorum] *regul*[arium] *S*[tockholm] *18. aprl. 1788.*

Charles Edward was again questioned about the Stuarts' connections with Freemasonry in 1787. The Lutheran theologian Friedrich Münter visited him and asked him about the subject, but the conversation quickly faltered because Charles Edward was so weak.[16] When he died on January 31, 1788, by virtue of this authentic Jacobite Masonic patent, his "coadjutor" Gustav III, "Eques a Corona Vindicata," succeeded him as leader of the "Order of the Knights of Saint John of the Temple." Did the King of Sweden nevertheless maintain some illusions about Charles Edward's Masonic powers? It is of course difficult to say. However, we know that as soon as he was informed of his death, he sent the Count of Fredenheim to his daughter in Italy. She gave him "a document in Latin" on July 19, 1788.[17]

---

16 Element reported by Frank McLynn in *Charles Edward Stuart*, 548, according to Frederik Münter, *Aus den Tagebuchern Friedrich Munters wandrrund lajahre eines Danisken gelerthen*, 3 vols. (Copenhagen and Leipzig: P. Haase, 1937), 2:232.

17 Nordmann, *Gustave III*, 220.

This forgotten episode, where Freemasonry furtively meets the debris of major history, is highly curious. However, like many curiosities, far from being anecdotal, it highlights remarkable traits of human psychology. It tells, after all, of just how powerful an idea can be—even if it is false. Opinion was convinced that the Stuarts were the secret leaders of the Lodges, and they eventually became just that, admittedly in somewhat unusual and, in truth, rather funny circumstances.

Since time immemorial, the question "Are you a Freemason?" has been answered according to Masonic instructions with the words "My Brothers recognize me as such." Charles Edward had long been recognized "as such" by many Masons during the eighteenth century. As his life drew to an end, he eventually accepted this crown that everyone wanted to place on his head—the only crown he ever had.

The Masonic Orders of the Holy Sepulcher in Eighteenth-Century France

We are a long way from Jerusalem! The few Chivalric Orders of the Middle Ages that still existed in the eighteenth century had become decorations, primarily a way of according pensions to the King's most faithful servants. In around 1730–1740, various Masonic circles wanted to recreate a true chivalric path, combining a new spiritual ideal with worldly action. This is the origin of Masonic chivalry and several of its High Degrees.[1] They wanted to put back together what history had scattered: the spirit and rites of chivalry. From the end of the Middle Ages to the Age of Enlightenment, the spirit of chivalry continued to thrive in a whole body of constantly read literature. As for the rites, we can still see them practiced in 1740, for example in the ceremonies of the Orders of Saint-Lazare or Malta. Indeed, a connection has been made between the Order of Saint-Lazare's receiving of Ramsay and his famous and highly successful oration in the Lodge. In this speech, Ramsay defends the idea of a line of descent between Medieval Chivalry and Freemasonry.

> *Our ancestors, the Crusaders, gathered together from all parts of Christendom in the Holy Land, desired thus to reunite into one sole Fraternity the individuals of all nations [... and] to form in the course of ages a spiritual empire*[2]*[...]. At the time of the Crusades in Palestine many*

---

1 This is the issue we attempted to clarify in our study: *La Chevalerie Maçonnique: Franc-maçonnerie, imaginaire chevaleresque et légende templière au siècle des Lumières*, (Paris: Editions Dervy Collection Renaissance Traditionnelle, 2005, 230 p.)

2 Andrew Michael Ramsay's oration, "Discours préliminaire pour servir d'introduction aux obligations" in Louis-François de La Tierce, *Histoire, Obligations et Statuts de la Très Vénérable Confraternité des Francs-Maçons...* (Francfort sur

*princes, lords and citizens associated themselves and vowed
to restore the Temple of the Christians in the Holy Land,
to employ themselves in bringing back their architecture to
its first institution. They agreed upon several ancient signs
and symbolic words drawn from the well of religion in order to recognize themselves amongst the heathen and the
Saracens. These signs and words were only communicated
to those who promised solemnly, even sometimes at the foot
of the altar, never to reveal them. This sacred promise was
therefore not an execrable oath, as it has been called, but
a respectable bond to unite Christians of all nationalities
in one confraternity. Some time after, our Order formed an
intimate union with the Knights of St. John of Jerusalem.
From that time our Lodges took the name of Lodges of St.
John. This union was made after the example set by the Israelites when they erected the second Temple who, whilst they
handled the trowel and mortar with one hand, in the other
held the sword and buckler.*[3]

Was it Ramsay who "launched the idea?" Or, as we think, did
he merely pass on a belief found in certain circles lying at the
roots of modern Freemasonry. Whatever the case may be, in the
1730s–1740s, the Lodges began practicing chivalric ceremonies
and giving Degrees of "Knight of the Orient" or "Knight Kadosh"
(in its primitive form of "Sublime Knight Elect"). The main model
that Masonic chivalry seeks to pick up on is of course the Order of
the Temple, with its prestige and its halo of mystery. Certain legend-
ary tales which accompany it and which legitimate the first Templar Degrees do in fact already refer to the Holy Sepulcher. Thus,

---

le Meyn: F. Varrentrapp, 1742), 129. La Tierce's text corresponds to the supposedly definitive version, or the "Grand Lodge" of the *Discours* (early 1737).
English version taken from http://www.freemasons-freemasonry.com/ram
say_biography_oration.html, consulted March 9, 2016.

3   Andrew Michael Ramsay's oration. English version taken from http://www.
freemasons-freemasonry.com/ramsay_biography_oration.html, consulted
March 9, 2016.

in the 1750s–1760s, a text entitled "De la Maçonnerie parmi les Chrétiens" ("On Masonry Among Christians"),[4] explained that the first Knights of the Temple were welcomed by the canons of the Holy Sepulcher and that these canons then united with the Templars, realizing that their mission was the same. This idea of the first canons of the Holy Sepulcher participating in the foundation of the Order of the Temple can be found in several Masonic systems of the eighteenth century, for example the famous and highly interesting "Clerks of the Temple" of the theosophist and crypto-Catholic pastor Johann August Starck.[5] However, from the 1760s, we find various documents containing the traces of a specific Masonic Degree of Knight of the Holy Sepulcher.

The Mythical Order of the Holy Sepulcher

The Order of the Holy Sepulcher is among the Great Orders born in the heart of the Middle Ages. Following the publication of André Favyn's *Théâtre d'Honneur et de Chevalerie* in 1620, the many treatises which, from the seventeenth to the early eighteenth century, report the history of the Orders of Chivalry all devote a significant chapter to it. Favyn explains that:

> *The Order of the Holy Sepulcher is the first and oldest of all those in Palestine and the Holy Land. The City of Jerusalem having been conquered from the Emperors of Greece by the Saracens, the Guard of the Holy Sepulcher & of the Mount Calvary were left by these Saracens to certain regular noble Canons.*
>
> *Godfrey of Bouillon, first King of Jerusalem and of the French Nation, did much good for the Canons [...].*
>
> *Baudouin, the first of his name, successor to his Brother Go-*

---

4 René Le Forestier, *La Franc-Maçonnerie Occultiste et Templière aux XVIIIe et XIXe siècles*, second edition published by Antoine Faivre with addenda and index, 2 volumes (Paris: La Table d'Emeraude, 1987), vol. I, 68.

5 Le Forestier, *La Franc-Maçonnerie Occultiste et Templière*, 157.

defroy, made these regular Canons (from the monks that they were) into men of arms & Knights of the Holy Sepulcher [...]. This institution was carried out by the aforementioned King Baudouin, in the year of Grace 1103. He gave them for leader & Grand Master the Patriarch of Jerusalem, to whom he granted the power to confer this Order.

The Pope Alexander VI of the name, in the fourth year of his Pontificate, & the year of Grace 1496, transported to the Holy See and to him the power to confer this Order of Knights of the Holy Sepulcher, & declared himself and his successors Popes, Chiefs and Sovereign Grand Masters of this Order, giving power to its Vicar General Guardian of the Holy Sepulcher (still of the rule of Saint Francis of Assisi) to confer the Order to Pilgrims & travelers of the Holy Land, married or not married, in exchange for their vowing on the aforementioned Holy Sepulcher that they are of Noble birth...[6]

However, a little further on Favyn, worthy apologist of the society of orders, which at the time was the basis of the French monarchy, laments that:

it has come about by necessity of the family of the Cordeliers of the Holy Sepulcher that the Guardian gives and confers this Order to any who requests it, without precise inquiry, or authentic testimonial concerning the nobility of the person presenting himself, in exchange for thirty sequins of gold, given to the Convent, such that most of the Knights of the Holy Sepulcher are commoners...

Thus, because of the symbolic power of the site, at the end of the Middle Ages, it became customary for noble (or less noble!) pilgrims to have themselves received as knights in the church of the Holy Sepulcher in Jerusalem. Consequently, unlike other great

---

6   André Favyn, *Le Théatre d'Honneur et de Chevalerie ou l'histoire des ordres militaires...*, (Paris: Robert Fouët, 1620), 1595–1598.

Orders such as "The Temple" or "the Hospital" (Malta), the Holy Sepulcher has no pyramid structure with commanderies and provinces. It is, in fact, more a tradition than a true Order. In 2004, Jean-Pierre de Gennes brought out a scholarly and well-researched study,[7] which became an important reference work. The author's first task is to show that, before the Pope established the "modern" Order of the Holy Sepulcher in 1847, in a way, contrary to everything written beforehand, although there had been Knights of the Holy Sepulcher since the Middle Ages, the Order of the Holy Sepulcher itself never really existed (in any case, not as an organization with its administrations and its hierarchy). One thing that encouraged confusion is that once they were back in Europe, these pilgrims who had become Knights of the Holy Sepulcher in Jerusalem often joined pious confraternities under the patronage of the Holy Sepulcher. Some of these confraternities, like that of Paris, became important organizations. In the eighteenth century, exploiting the reduced vigilance of the public authorities regarding these matters, a few individuals were quick to confer Knighthood of the Holy Sepulcher themselves, but this time in Paris, Lyon, or Marseille.

From the 1760s, the whole strategy of the Parisian Fraternity of the Holy Sepulcher consisted in trying to obtain recognition as an order of chivalry, particularly from the royal authorities. In a few cases, the Knights of the Holy Sepulcher that we find in France in the eighteenth century were therefore received during a pilgrimage to Jerusalem, by the Franciscans who since the Middle Ages had guarded the holy places. However, in most cases they were received in one of the major Fraternities of the Holy Sepulcher, found in several cities. What unites them is their shared reference to the mythical Order of the Holy Sepulcher, the story of which is reported in many treatises on the Orders of Chivalry. These were one of the most fertile sources of the chivalric imagination in the Age of Enlightenment. An anecdote reported by Tschoudy in his classic 1766 work, *L'Étoile Flamboyante*, shows that there were many Masons in

---

7   Jean-Pierre de Gennes, *Les Chevaliers du Saint-Sépulcre de Jérusalem* (Versailles: Editions Mémoire & Documents, 2004), vol. 1, 481 p., vol. 2, 507 p. + 567 p.

the Parisian archconfraternity of the Holy Sepulcher.[8] This may be the origin of the Masonic Degree of Knight of the Holy Sepulcher.

The Masonic Degree of Knight of the Holy Sepulcher in around 1760

The 1760–1770 decade appears to have been particularly fertile and creative in terms of the High Degrees, especially the Chivalric High Degrees. Although we cannot precisely date it, we can identify a Degree of "Knight of the Holy Sepulcher" which seems to appear in the 1760s, in various manuscript collections[9] of rituals:

> *This reception is respectable because it is established to support the faith and because the order is the first origin of the first Masons who were Canons in rule.*
>
> *The Chapter is draped in red, as are the throne and altar.*
>
> *The tracing board in the center represents the sepulcher of J∴ C∴ [with] an angel above pointing to the sky with its index finger.*
>
> *Around the tracing board are twenty lights placed at the four corners of the tomb, in groups of five forming triangles.*
>
> *To the North, the closed Sepulcher is represented, the Sword of Godfrey of Bouillon is placed on top, with his spurs and*

---

8   *"A confrere from Jerusalem died a little while ago. He was a Freemason, the Master of the Confraternity that year was also a Freemason; at the funeral ceremony, which all the confreres attended, the question arose of who would be the pallbearers [...] the Master assigned these sought-after roles to Freemasons..."* [Baron de Tschoudy], *L'Étoile Flamboyante ou la société des francs-maçons considérée sous tous les aspects* (Paris: Antoine Boudet, 1766), 63. The "Confraternity of Jerusalem" was the abridged name for the Parisian archconfraternity of the "Knights, Pilgrims and Travelers of the Holy Sepulcher of Jerusalem"; see: *Ancien statut de l'Ordre Hospitalier et Militaire du Saint Sépulcre de Jérusalem* (Paris, Cailleau, 1776), 174–184.

9   For example, in the Manuscript Cabinet at the National Library of France (BnF), the documents: NAF 10958, f°185-197; Baylot FM⁴ 103; FM⁴ 1046⁽ᶜ⁾. Aside from a few copy errors, all of these manuscripts describe the same ritual.

*his gold collar of the Order, on the end of which hangs a gold
Jerusalem cross.*

*The Respectable Grand Master is dressed in prelate's cloth-
ing and the whole assembly is dressed in black, with white
gloves and aprons.[10]*

Upon the opening of the works, the Grand Master asks:

Why were you received as a Kgt of the Holy Sepulcher?

- To fight the enemies of the Faith

What brings us together in this holy place?

- Honor, strength, and wisdom.

*My dear noble knight brothers, let us practice with fervor
the three principles of virtue, the Chapter is open, let us act
there with the decency due to this great mystery.*

The reception of the new Mason Knight of the Holy Sepulcher
is quite simple. The recipient is brought into the Chapter and the
"tracing board" (the symbolic representation of the Holy Sepulcher at the center of the Lodge) is unveiled to him. Then the Grand
Master knights him before the assembly with a sword, which he is
told is the sword of Godfrey of Bouillon. The Masonic ceremony
basically follows that described by Favyn and several other authors
of *Treatises* in their chapters on the Order of the Holy Sepulcher,
including the giving of the spurs. In conclusion, again as stipulated
in Favyn, the recipient is given the insignia of the order: the classic
cross of Jerusalem. The duty sworn by the new Knight clearly shows
the ethos of the Degree:

*I swear to fight the enemies of the Apostolic and Roman
Catholic faith, to respect the prelates of the Church, to
support the arms of my prince; and, should the Christian*

---

10 *Collection maçonnique, 5ᵉ partie, Les Chevaliers du Sᵗ Sépulcre, 7–24. Library
   of the Grand Orient de France, A.R. 5330.

princes go to war to fight the enemies of our Holy Religion in the Holy Land, I commit to be there in person, or if I am prevented from doing so, to send another worthy of fulfilling the vow I have made.

As for many vows proposed upon obtaining Degrees, the formulas should undoubtedly not be taken literally, even in the eighteenth century, as their role is primarily symbolic. That said, the Degree of Knight of the Holy Sepulcher clearly belongs to the family of the Christian High Degrees. This family is still represented by the Rectified Scottish Regime today, using very different methods. In the eighteenth century, there was a somewhat marginal current of High Degrees, presenting themselves as a defense and illustration of the Christian faith in a Masonic context. Examples include the Knights of the Aurora and of Palestine, or the Knights of the Triple Cross. These Degrees remain symbolically connected to the medieval chivalry of the Holy Land seen, following Ramsay, as the origin of Freemasonry. The particularity of this first Masonic Knight of the Holy Sepulcher is that it goes further by proclaiming itself Catholic. This is a curious claim, when we consider that the Pope excommunicated Freemasons from 1738. However, this excommunication had little effect in France before the revolution. The parliaments did not "record" it, so it could not lawfully be applied to French Masons. For our part, we will interpret this claim of Catholicism as a will to connect Freemasonry to medieval Christianity. We do not know how this Degree of Knight of the Holy Sepulcher was practiced originally or in the 1760s. It is probable that like many High Degrees, it was conferred after various other Degrees, depending on the meetings of its promoters and the Lodges they visited or frequented. The Degree itself proposes no specific esoteric teaching, but the simple fact of putting the recipient, in spirit, in the presence of the Holy Sepulcher naturally had a strong spiritual dimension for an eighteenth-century man with his mind full of Christian references.

Pierre-François Isnard's Masonic Order of the Holy Sepulcher in 1780

Although between 1760 and 1780 we find scattered traces of a Degree of Knight of the Holy Sepulcher being practiced in a Masonic context, from 1780, we discover the existence of a specific Masonic order, with the Knight of the Holy Sepulcher as its cornerstone. This true Masonic Order of the Holy Sepulcher was, in particular, active in Strasbourg and Toulon, and its leader is known: Pierre-François Isnard.

Pierre-François Isnard, from Strasbourg, was a very committed Mason from the 1750s to the early nineteenth century. Born in 1727,[11] the son of an engraver, he was a soldier from 1747 to 1777, a lieutenant of Dragoons (specifically in the Legion of Lorraine and in the Berry-Cavalerie), and a Knight of Saint-Louis. A poet and at times a writer,[12] he participated in various literary circles, but is also known as an author of uniform collections. He is also thought to be the father of the classic *Petits soldats de Strasbourg* ("Little Soldiers of Strasbourg"). He died in the Alsace capital in 1807. Received as a Mason at a very young age, in around 1753,[13] he founded the Strasbourg Lodge *Le Parfait Silence*, on February 4, 1764. This Lodge, which remained active (with its ups and downs) until the Revolution, originally had a heavy contingent of soldiers and nobles. Its tumultuous history was the product of disputes between these Brothers and those from the bourgeoisie.

---

11 See the entry on this by François Lotz on page 1758 of the *Nouveau dictionnaire de biographie alsacienne*; H. Haug, "Trois artistes méridionaux à Strasbourg au XVIIIe siècle," 113–170. Entry on François Isnard (v. 1699–1765), P.F. Isnard (1727-1807) and P.M. Isnard (1723–1795), the first two of whom were engravers and the latter an architect, in *Archives alsaciennes d'histoire de l'art*, 6ᵉ année, (Strasbourg: Imprimerie strasbourgeoise, 1927).

12 The BnF manuscripts cabinet contains under shelf-mark NAF 6456, *Lettres et poésie de Pierre-François Isnard, officier de Dragons en retraite à Strasbourg (1799–1805), XVIIIᵉ-XIXᵉ siècles*, Pap, 80 sheets.

13 In a letter to the Grand Orient, in 1789, he writes that he *"worked for 36 years for the glory of the Order."* (BnF, FM² 426, f°102) This means he entered the Lodge in 1753.

In the Masonic system promoted and spread by Isnard, the Degree of Knight of the Holy Sepulcher appears as the final Degree of the Rose-Croix Chapter, of which it is a sort of "Inner Order." From 1750 to the Revolution, the "Rose-Croix" often represents the end of the Masonic path. It is a very specific Degree, because after "discovering" the three theological virtues and "a new law," the candidate is invited to relive *allegorically the events of the death and resurrection of Jesus Christ.* The whole ceremony is of course steeped in a highly religious atmosphere, and probably aims to reconnect with what was imagined to be primitive Christianity,[14] one of the great myths which haunted the eighteenth and nineteenth centuries. It is pointless to emphasize that in the Age of the Enlightenment, the Rose-Croix was the ultimate Christian Masonic Degree. In 1763, the ritual of the Marquis de Gages even specifies that "*he takes the title of Christian knight.*"[15]

The Knight of the Holy Sepulcher therefore fits naturally into this context. However, beyond a shared symbolic atmosphere, the consistency between the two Degrees is even stronger, because the last sequence in the ritual of the Rose-Croix is held in front of "*the tomb and the instant of the Resurrection of Jesus Christ [...] and, on the altar, which is well decorated, is the representation of Jesus Christ emerging triumphant from his tomb.*" By being *ultimately* received as a Knight of the Holy Sepulcher, the Knight of the Rose-Croix participates symbolically in the end of the story. He is instituted as guardian of the tomb, the highly sacred and holy nature of which has been revealed to him as a Knight of the Rose-Croix.

It is therefore in a real "symbolic logic" that Isnard makes the Knight of the Holy Sepulcher the inner Order of the Chapter of the Rose-Croix. In fact:

> *Art. 4: There will be two types of members in the chapter, and these will be the knights of the R∴ + ∴ And the kgts∴ who have passed into the Degree of Kgt∴ of the Benevo-*

14 See Chapter VI.
15 BnF, FM⁴ 79, f°101 v°.

lence of the Holy City of the Holy Sepulcher of Jerusalem in Palestine.[16]

We were able to identify the texts used by Pierre-François Isnard's Masonic Order of the Holy Sepulcher. Thus, the collection BnF NAF 10956 (ff.° 228-237) gives a very full copy of the ritual of "Knight of Benevolence of the Holy City and the Holy Sepulcher." The "lodge tracing board" features a large image of the Holy Sepulcher in the center of the Chapter. This is presided over by a Commander, who proclaims:

> *In the name of God the all-powerful Master of the Universe & by the permission of our legitimate superiors, I open this assembly.*

The Brother Procurator then announces:

> *Entry is permitted to any free man who comes for Faith and by Charity in the silence of hope [...], Brother Commander, a Knight of the Rose-Croix solicits the honor of being employed in the guard of the Holy Sepulcher [...]. He comes from Judea, he has come via Nazareth, Rafael led him, and he is of the tribe of Judah.*

The Commander then counsels the candidate on the nobility of Benevolence and of "*The Order of chivalry into which you have just entered & which is founded on our divine religion & the exercise of social and patriotic virtues.*" After the candidate has asserted their determination to follow the path of Benevolence and join the Order, the Commander declares:

> *The veil of symbols will fall & the Masonic shadows which*

---

16 *Règlement pour le Chapitre R∴ + ∴. A l'orient de Toulon approuvé le 13 avril 1786,* BnF, Manuscrits Cabinet, Fonds maçonnique/Masonic collection, archives of the Grand Orient de France, Dossier on the Lodges of Toulon, FM² 438. We only know this regulation from the copy made by the Brothers of Toulon in 1802, for the revival of the Chapter, as the eighteenth century texts have disappeared. The Toulon copy explains that it is faithful in all points to the text transmitted by Strasbourg.

surround you will disappear & you will know the respectable order which has perpetuated its existence through Masonry.

The recipient then pledges loyalty to the Order and the Commander makes a short speech to him, where following Ramsay, he explains the connections which unite the Temple of Solomon, the desert hermits, the first chivalry and the Freemasonry which served as a refuge for the persecuted or pursued Knights. All these institutions having over time and according to the circumstances arbitrated *"The safekeeping of the primitive science of man preserved in the ancient mysteries."*

Then comes the knighting, which repeats the first Degree of the Knight of the Holy Sepulcher described above, and then the classic entrance ceremony for the Order of the Holy Sepulcher as described in treatises on the Orders of Chivalry. The Commander announces:

> *Upon the order of my Brethren & fellows & you my Brother, repeat with me:*
>
> *I ... promise to God, to our L.J.C. & to the blessed virgin Mary that I will religiously observe with all my power the rules of the Order, as a true soldier of J∴C∴.*

He puts the sword in his hand with the words:

> *Be loyal, hardy, good & strong, Kgt of the Benevolence of the Holy City & of the Holy Sepulcher of our L∴J∴C∴ so that with his elect he might deign to place you and gather you in his heavenly court. Amen.*

Giving him the spurs, he says:

> *Take these spurs for the salvation of he who helps you so that you can reach the Holy City, walk around it & contribute to the Guard of the Holy Sepulcher.*

He takes the sword and gives it back to the candidate:

> *Receive this sword in the name of the father, the son & the Holy Spirit; use it to defend the Holy Church & to confound*

the enemy of the cross of J∴C∴ & of the Christian faith; offend no-one unless authorized in the name of he who lives and reigns &c. Amen.

He re-sheaths the sword:

Gird yourself with this sword. Let it hang at your thigh in the name of our L∴J∴C∴ & know that the Saints did not win the kingdoms with swords but with faith.

At this point, the candidate draws his sword and gives it to the Commander, then kneels, bowing, placing himself before the sign of the good shepherd, he says:

Deus protector meus

The Commander makes him a knight using these words:

I make and create you a Kgt∴ of the Benevolence of the Holy City & of the very Holy Sepulcher of our Lord J∴C∴ in the name of the Father & the Son & the Holy Spirit, Amen.

The Commander kisses his forehead:

Receive the sign of the order so that in carrying it you will always be a victor. Lord God, by this sign deliver us from our enemies. Amen.

Finally, giving him the shield, he says:

My brother, finish arming yourself; kgt∴ receive the shield of knowledge to help you ward off the blows of the ungodly.

Then he gives him the lance, adding:

This lance must serve you against the enemies of God, the Prince, the Fatherland, your Mason Brethren and the Order as a whole. By giving you the accolade, I separate you from the corrupt world, from the path of the evildoers & ungodliness. Live for justice and for truth. Let the Very High

law be engraved in your heart so that you might meditate
on it every day of your life.

And since we are, after all, in a Masonic context, the Commander then gives the new Knight the signs, words and grips of the Degree. The "sacred word" is "Melchizedek." After a prayer and another exhortation to fulfil the duties "of the first Christian knights," the orator of the Chapter reads a long "historic speech." This explanation reveals that the Knights of the Holy Sepulcher and Masons are simply two successive veils to conceal the true nature of the Order which is none other than that of the Templars. The text uses classic elements from the discourse of the Templar High Degrees of the eighteenth century. The great riches which were at the origin of the persecution of the Templars by Philip the Fair were just a consequence of their esoteric knowledge. In fact:

Hugues de Payens & the first Templars worked to repair
the house given to them by Baudoin II in the Temple. They
searched the ruins to take materials from them. While
searching, they came across an iron box containing, among
other precious things, the process to achieve the great work.

A few Knights survived the suppression of the Order and managed to preserve the "great secret." After fleeing for a long time, they found refuge in Scotland, where they were welcomed by the Knights of Saint Andrew. Then, to evade all danger, they joined the Masons, whose secret Lodges offered the ideal shelter.

You are too prudent not to see how essential it is to hide our
operations & even our name. This is why we bear the name
of Benevolence of the Holy City under the allegory of the
Holy Sepulcher of Jerusalem.

After the prayer and the incensation of the Chapter, which follows the historical speech, the Commander says:

My Brethren, let us disguise ourselves as Masons to better
hide our state & ensure our survival, to hide our motives

from our enemies, let us take for emblems the name, the cus-
toms and the tools of the Masons who have served us for 478
years.[17] Transierunt vetera a cuncta nova facta sunt.

Here, all remove the costume of Kgts∴ & dress as Ma-
sons. Five Brothers take the tools of Masonry & walk a lap
around the temple.

After a short speech on the symbolism of the phoenix and the
pelican, the Commander closes the works of the Chapter.

As in the Degree of the Holy Sepulcher of the 1760s which
served as its basis, the Knight of Benevolence of the Holy City of the
Holy Sepulcher must profess "the Apostolic and Roman Catholic
religion." Even more curiously, in the "historical speech" for the Degree, the Pope's responsibility in the persecutions against the Order
of the Temple is not played down. Perhaps this high claim to Catholicism should actually be placed in parallel with the internal controversies of Strasbourg Masonry. It is not impossible that behind the
proclaimed equality, the religious divisions between Protestants and
Catholics also overlaid social and cultural divisions, for example between soldiers or civil servants "from inside" (as they say in Alsace!)
and from mainly Lutheran Strasbourg men. This hypothesis is based,
in particular, on the full name of Isnard's Degree of the Holy Sepulcher: "Knight of Benevolence of the Holy City of the Holy Sepulcher of Jerusalem in Palestine." This name unambiguously betrays a
rivalry, or at least a positioning, in relation to the great Strasbourg
Masonic system of the 1770s to 1780s: The Benevolent Knights
of the Holy City, Inner Order of the Rectified Scottish Regime...
a Rectified Scottish Regime whose leaders in Strasbourg were great
Lutheran nobles such as the Turckheims or the Saltzmanns.

Isnard's Masonic Order of the Holy Sepulcher seems to have
been active in the mid-1780s. Due to its somewhat marginal position in relation to the major Masonic organizations, we have few
traces of it. The copies made at the start of the nineteenth century

---

17 This allows us to date the original of our copy to 1785: 1307 (arrest of the
   Templars by Philip the Fair), plus 478 years, gives us 1785.

by the Chapter of Toulon testify to the existence of this Chapter and the "father" Chapter of Strasbourg. Were there others? Possibly, but in any case, it was a small Masonic system which probably never had more than a few dozen Knights. We should note the presence of several Knights of Malta in the Chapter of Toulon, for example the young Aimé de Framond, whose diploma has been preserved and who trained in the port as a "Naval Guard." This is unsurprising, because in France at the time, almost 20% of Knights of Malta were Masons. Elsewhere in our work, we have shown the close links between Freemasonry and the Order of Malta in the eighteenth century.[18] We can add to this that the Order had women's Lodges, "of adoption" (to use the classic terminology), of which we know one "Ritual for the adoption of Women in the Order of Chivalry of Benevolence under the allegory of the Holy Sepulcher of Jerusalem in Palestine."[19]

What is evident in Isnard's Order is this will to establish a connection to the founding legend described by Ramsay in his speech in the mid-1730s. Freemasonry maintains close relationships with Chivalry, or in any case with this spiritual and "initiatory" Chivalry which, in the heart of the Middle Ages and in the Holy Land, sheltered a Christianity closer to its (particularly Jewish, and in part esoteric) sources. The fact that this had only a distant connection with historical reality is ultimately secondary. The Mason Knight received not a history lesson, but a founding legend which had to make sense. After Ramsay in 1736, Tschoudy would, in 1766 in his work *L'Etoile Flamboyante*, be the great apologist of a chivalric and Christian Masonry. For Tschoudy, after the three Degrees of Apprentice, Fellow, and Master, Freemasonry concentrated its teachings in two High Degrees. The Scot of Saint Andrew of Scotland and the Knight of the Aurora and of Palestine. This latter degree, directly derived from the Medieval Chivalry of the Holy Land, offers the ultimate teachings of the Order. "*The Knights of Palestine are thus the first and the true Masons,*" Tschoudy tells us. A further clue of this is the Masonic

---

18 See Chapter VIII.

19 BnF, NAF 10958, f°179–184.

Order of the Holy Sepulcher's connection to Ramsay and Tschoudy: in the diplomas that he delivers, Isnard presents himself as "Knight of the Holy Sepulcher, Commander of Palestine."

In 1802, the Toulon Brothers tried to revive the Chapter of the *Perfect Silence*. After various events, they finally succeeded. However, the Degree of the Holy Sepulcher fell into disuse, and the *Perfect Silence* became a classic Rose-Croix Chapter without its "inner Order." In the great inventory of the High Degrees compiled by the Metropolitan Sovereign Chapter of the French Rite in 1807, Knight of the Holy Sepulcher is listed in the 6th series of the 5th Order, as the 50th Degree.[20] However, the "Arch of the 5th Order" is more a collection of rituals for study than a true site for the initiatory implementation of the Degrees. In any case, the 5th Order in turn died out in 1813. Yet the Masonic Degree of the Holy Sepulcher did not disappear.[21] Its trace can be found right at the end of the eighteenth century in the United States! We thus find it mentioned in the great revelation of David Bernard, *Light on Masonry*,[22] which came out in 1829, but includes many rituals from the end of the eighteenth century that were still in use at the start of the nineteenth. It is likely that the Masonic Knight of the Holy Sepulcher crossed the Atlantic via Toulon, Marseille or Bordeaux in the baggage of traveling Masons. It is worth emphasizing that the Irish played a major role in American Masonry of the High Degrees, and that there were quite

---

20 *Chevalier du Saint Sépulcre, 50ᵉ grade, 6ᵉ* série, BnF, FM⁴ 1046.[E]

21 Also worthy of our attention is the attempted creation of an Order of the Holy Sepulcher, with a few survivors of the eighteenth-century Parisian archconfraternity led by the Admiral Count Allemand at the start of Louis XVIII's reign. Jean-Pierre de Gennes wrote a history of this ("Une résurgence éphémère de l'Ordre sous la Restauration," in *Les Chevaliers du Saint-Sépulcre de Jérusalem*, volume II, second part, 261–387) and emphasized the many connections with Freemasonry. In fact, almost all of its members and leaders were Masons, particularly from the *Admirers of the Universe* Lodge. The quaint thing is that in 1847, the creators of the pontifical Order used elements coming from the (crypto-Masonic) Allemand's Order of the Holy Sepulcher.

22 David Bernard, "Knights of the Holy Sepulchre," in *Light on Masonry, a collection of all the most important documents on the subject of speculative Free masonry...* (Utica: William Williams, 182), 170–178.

a lot of Irish people in the French ports. From the United States, the Degree of "Knight of the Holy Sepulcher" was transported to England, undoubtedly by British soldiers returning from the American wars in around 1790.[23] It seems to have been practiced around Thomas Dunckerley with a collection of Christian chivalric High Degrees: Knight Templar, Knight of Malta and Knight of the Red Cross. This is the first time that we see the Knight of the Holy Sepulcher associated with the Degree of the Red Cross of Constantine. This association also appears in the papers of Alexander Dalziel in the 1830s. The Knight of the Holy Sepulcher thus continued to be practiced in the few small Masonic circles which maintained the Christian chivalric High degrees during the long Grand Mastery of the Duke of Sussex, who was very hostile to them. In 1865, Robert Wentworth Little organized the "modern" Grand Conclave of the Knights of the Red Cross of Constantine, of which the Knight of the Holy Sepulcher became an "appendant order." From the nineteenth century to the present day, it is still practiced in this context, including in France.

---

23 See: *The history and origin of the Masonic and Military Order of the Red Cross of Constantine and the appendant order of the Holy Sepulchre and of St. John the Evangelist: an analytical Survey* (London: published under the authority of the Grand Imperial Conclave, 1971).

Election, Representation, and Democracy: Debates Surrounding the Organization of the Grand Orient de France (1773–1789)

The position of the lodges during the Enlightenment and the French Revolution is a classic question in the eighteenth-century historiography. Initially denounced by certain counterrevolutionaries, the connection of Freemasonry to the events of 1789–1793 was later claimed by the Republican Brothers at the end of the nineteenth century. However, from Mathiez to Alain Le Bihan and Pierre Chevallier, the professional historians of the twentieth century ultimately challenged the idea that Freemasonry had played any real role in the revolutionary storm, dismissing the lodges as simple societies of banquets and festivities. The debate has been taken up again over the last 20 years with the works of Ran Halévy[1] and Margaret Jacob.[2] According to slightly different modalities, both give it an important role in the implementation and spread of a democratic social practice that prepared the way for political modernity. Thus, in *Living the Enlightenment*, Margaret Jacob emphasizes all the work the lodges undertook concerning their own organization. She shows how a group's collective reflection concerning the authority it submits to and the rules it applies to itself signal a different conception of public space and thus dissimulates a social work that is in fact political. Her research is based on a series of case studies in several European countries, and critics have at times underscored the selective nature of her examples. Thus *a contrario*, how can we analyze the phenomenon of the Templar Strict Observance, if not

---

1 Ran Halévi, *Les Loges maçonniques dans la France d'Ancien Régime aux origines de la sociabilité démocratique* (Paris: Cahier des Annales, Librairie Armand Colin, 1984).

2 Margaret C. Jacob, *Living the Enlightenment, Freemasonry and Politics in Eighteenth-century Europe* (New York/Oxford: Oxford University Press, 1991).

as a reaction by the nobility, which would seem to be a far cry from any democratic learning process? In this article, we would like to examine an episode of French Masonic history during which the success of the concept of "democratic social practice" seems particularly ripe for analysis. It involves debates on the statutes and rules of the Grand Orient de France that took place in Paris between 1773 and 1789. This study of a case which until now has remained in the shadows offers several advantages. First, it does not simply involve one Masonic group among others, but is the reflection of a body that brought together almost all French Freemasons. Second, throughout those 20 years, the officials of the Grand Orient would be led to clarify, modify, and make changes to these internal rules depending on the circumstances. We are thus able to witness how a collective rule is debated and constructed over time during the last decades of the *Ancien Régime*. Finally, since all of the archives have been preserved, we have a very large set of documents on the development of rules as well as on their later implementation in the different bodies. An additional interest, aside from the persons and individual futures in the *bourgeoisie de robes* or the liberal nobility, is that the officials of the Grand Orient undoubtedly belonged to the social classes that would launch the Revolution. Given the breadth of the topic, in this article we will limit ourselves to drawing attention to this veritable mine for historiography, present points of reference, and suggest a few directions for future work.

1728–1773: French Masonic Authority Struggles to Organize

From its introduction to Paris around 1725 until the end of the 1760s, French Freemasonry would repeatedly endeavor to organize itself. It first recognized the authority of a Grand Master for France in 1728,[3] thereby freeing itself from English tutelage. In 1735, it endowed itself with statutes, establishing a Grand Lodge for the first

---

3   See Alain Le Bihan, Paris: 1728, "Les maçons et les Grands Maîtres jacobites ou la reconnaissance du premier d'entre eux: le Duc de Wharton," in *Les plus belles pages de la Franc-maçonnerie française* (Paris: Dervy, 2003), 36-37.

time.[4] However, this First Grand Lodge did not seem to hold much authority over the lodges of the Kingdom. At regular intervals—June 24, 1745; July 4, 1755; May 19, 1760; and April 17, 1763[5]—it would try to establish its supremacy by promulgating statutes. Each of these texts insists on the authority it claims to have over the lodges of the kingdom, but to little effect. Until the 1760s, the lodges existed in semi-independence. Older lodges established newer ones and each corresponded with various others, depending on the circumstances. The unity of French Freemasonry could only be found in the fact that all recognized the Grand Master. From 1743 to 1771, he would be a prominent figure in Louis XV's France, namely, the Count of Clermont, a *prince du sang*. However, the rule of Louis de Bourbon-Condé was only a symbolic patronage and relatively distant, as was the custom during the *Ancien Régime*; the Grand Master never intervened in the management of the Order. It was, however, in his name that, in 1761, the first real attempt was made to establish a central authority over the lodges. Through a substitute appointed by the Grand Master, Augustin Chaillon de Jonville, the Grand Lodge came to life and the lodges of the kingdom were informed that they would then have to pledge allegiance to it. However, the "awoken" Grand Lodge was populated solely by Parisians, and the provinces complained about recognizing the "Grand Lodge of Masters of Paris said to be of France,"[6] according to the brothers from Lyon. It was challenged and quickly split into different factions, and again interrupted its work in 1766. The death of the Count of Clermont in 1771 and the need to elect a successor brought about a new meeting of the Grand Lodge.

---

4 See Etienne Fournial, *Les plus anciens devoirs et règlements de la Franc-maçonnerie française, Annales du Grand Orient de France—Supplément au n°48 du Bulletin du G∴O∴ de France* (Paris: n.p., 1964); new edition, *Renaissance Traditionnelle* 134 (April 2003).

5 These texts are published in: Alain Le Bihan, *Francs-maçons et ateliers parisiens de la Grande Loge de France au XVIIIe siècle (1760–1795)* (Paris: Bibliothèque Nationale, 1973).

6 BnF, FM[1] 111 a, folio 35, cited by René Désaguliers in "La Grande Loge de Paris dite de France et les "autres grades" de 1756 à 1766," *Renaissance Traditionnelle* 89 (January 1992): 14.

The Formation of the Grand Orient:
A Crisis in Representation?

The events that would lead to the formation of the Grand Orient de France thus begin like a classic episode of the *Ancien Régime*—with the gathering of notable figures to solicit a protector—and would in a few weeks be transformed into a "National Assembly" of elected deputies.[7] After the death of the Count of Clermont, a minority faction of the former Grand Lodge attempted to reestablish its audience and skillfully offered the leadership of the order to the Duke of Montmorency-Luxembourg. It was also agreed that the Grand Mastership would be offered to the Duke of Chartre, cousin of the King, future head of the house of Orléans and thus the noble with the highest rank in the kingdom after his father; a candidate who could not be contested. He accepted, which made any real opposition to the process that began impossible. It would be delayed, however, for a few months due to the momentary disgrace of Philippe d'Orléans, who was removed from the Court for opposing parliamentary reform. Parisian Masonic circles began to agitate and a group reunited around the new "Administrator General" (such is the title adopted by the Duke of Montmorency-Luxembourg) proposed a long list of reforms to finally give French Freemasonry a truly shared organization.

The main obstacle remained the majority faction of the former Grand Lodge that was not associated with these events. Montmorency-Luxembourg's entire strategy would be to marginalize it by challenging its representativeness; traditional authority would be countered with representative authority. For this, principles would

---

7   For a presentation that is both specific and inclusive of the fairly complex process that would lead to the formation of the Grand Orient de France, see Pierre Chevallier, *Histoire de la Franc-maçonnerie, I—La Maçonnerie Ecole de l'Egalité (1725–1799)* (Paris: Fayard, 1974), 151–176. To follow the details of these operations see *Constitution du Grand Orient de France par la Grande Loge Nationale—1773*, introduction by Arthur Groussier (Paris: Gloton, 1931), which transcribes all the minutes of the meetings and several appendices; and Daniel Kerjan, *Les Débuts de la franc-maçonnerie française, de la Grande Loge au Grand Orient, 1688–1793* (Paris: Devy, 2013).

be proposed whose application would go well beyond the scope of Freemasonry. The replacement of officials and the implementation of a new Masonic administration implied the adoption of new statutes. The rules of 1763 appeared obsolete, and the former Grand Lodge had itself changed its reference texts several times. New statutes were thus prepared by a commission in close collaboration with Montmorency-Luxembourg. Officially, of course, it was simply a question of *"reforming abuses returning the royal art to its former splendor and luster."*[8] The challenge for the different assemblies would be to adopt these new statutes which would validate the reform orchestrated by the Administrator General. Beginning in Chapter 1, two articles point to a small revolution in terms of the customs of the former Grand Lodge. Article 4 of Section 1 states: *"The Grand Orient de France will forthwith only recognize as Lodge Worshipful Master [president] the Master raised to this rank by the free choice of the Members of the Lodge."* This marked the end of the "irremovable" Worshipful Master who held their presidency "for life," which was how any particular office was held at the time. Election became the norm and would be applied to all Masonic functions. The Grand Master and the Administrator General set the example by vacating their initial appointment by the officials of the Grand Lodge, and by presenting themselves for election, bringing together representatives from all the lodges. Not only did the Administrator General, the First Christian Baron of France, submit to the election, but he also agreed to enter into the debate arena with the good bourgeois of the former Grand Lodge, who were decided to ask high price for their sacrifice. The second key innovation: *"The Grand Orient de France shall be constituted of [...] all the current Worshipful Master or Deputies of the Lodges, both in Paris and in the Provinces"* (Chapter 1, Section 2, Article 1). All the lodges would thus be represented in the new administration of the Order. Seeing that they were offered a share of power, the delegates of the provincial lodges, who had been somewhat distrustful at first, in the end rallied to the reform and became its main supporters. The members

---

8   Assembly of known deputies of the LL∴ of Province on March 8, 1773, in *Constitution du Grand Orient de France*, 47.

from Lyon who 10 years earlier had chastised *"the Grand Lodge of the Masters of Paris said to be of France"* hailed the *"National Assembly"*[9] of Lodges. This expression was used several times during the discussions in Paris. The debates, followed by the gradual adoption of the new statutes by the deputies of the lodges in Paris and the provinces, established the legitimacy of the new Grand Orient and the authority of the Duke of Montmorency-Luxembourg over the Order. It also gave French Freemasonry a new organization. The "Government of the Order" depended on three chambers: the Chamber of Administration, the Chamber of Paris, and the Chamber of the Provinces. As their names suggest, the first guaranteed the management of the central organization and especially finances, while the other two managed the lodges in terms of their respective constituencies (Constitutions, certificates, various disputes, etc.). The members of these bodies were all elected from within the assembly of the deputies of the lodges because:

> *"The forty-five current officers shall always be up for the election of the Grand Orient; one-third shall be renewed every year [...] and chosen in the Grand Orient."*[10]

In a few months, these meetings bringing together representatives of the enlightened bourgeoisie—such as Lalande or Guillotin—and the liberal nobility—such as Montmorency-Luxembourg and his friends—would set up an organization that was radically different from the former Grand Lodge. Principles in place at the new Grand Orient de France, such as the relative separation of powers,[11] elections, and representation at all levels, were no doubt inspired by the ideas of the Enlightenment which were for the first time applied within the eighteenth-century France. Pierre Chevallier shrewdly remarked: *"The Masonic Constituent Assembly that was the National*

---

9 Letter from the lodges of Lyon to their deputy Bacon de la Chevalerie, *Constitution du Grand Orient de France*, 174.

10 Statute of the Royal Order of Freemasonry, Chapter 2, Section 2, Article 1, in *Constitution du Grand Orient de France*, 238.

11 Finally, we could also point out the decisions concerning the different chambers, especially in matters of dispute, by a "Managing Board."

Grand Lodge would end its sessions on September 1, 1773. Without seeking to make an excessive comparison with the General Assemblies of 1789, one cannot, however, help but take note of the similarities that reveal a shared mindset."[12]

The "Democratic" Life of the Grand Orient from 1773 to 1793

Texts are one thing, but practices are something else. How would these "statutes of the Enlightenment" be applied in the daily operation of the Grand Orient? Numerous registers of the minutes of the various bodies of the Order show that the dignitaries really played the game of their liberal, pre-democratic rules. There are many examples, but here are just a few. At the opening of the assembly of the Grand Orient that took place 10 times a year, the president asks:

> *"...whether some deputies [have] requests to make for the LL∴ they represent."*[13]

Persons regularly had to be appointed to vacant positions and the election always seemed fairly open. Such was the case on May 19, 1786, for the important positions of First Grand Surveillants:

> *"The V∴D∴B∴ Duke de Crussol was appointed by a plurality of twenty-eight votes, the V∴F∴ Marquis de Vichy received six, and the B∴ Count de Roure one. Three were found to be blank."*[14]

The nobility, dukes, marquis, and counts submitted to the election of Brothers Sue, Carrel, Martin, Robin, etc.—all bourgeois.

As "policy" documents, the statutes of 1773 first aimed at unifying the lodges around a few principles and a new team. In the daily existence of the association, over the years and as problems arose, a

---

12 Chevallier, *Histoire de la Franc-maçonnerie*, 166.

13 For example, during the 162nd assembly of the G∴O∴ on August 19, 1785, BnF FM¹ 16, folio 181.

14 169th assembly of the G∴O∴, May 19, 1786, BnF FM¹ 16, folio 251, back.

certain number of clarifications would have to be made to the operations of the bodies of the Order. The chambers of the Grand Orient
were thus led to develop supplementary rules. All these regulatory
changes were not simply technical adjustments—far from it. Thus,
beginning in 1775, it was decided that the two main leaders of the
Grand Orient, the Administrator General and the Grand Conser-
vator, would be subject to election: previously, the individuals in
these roles had held them permanently once initially elected. In addition, in the very language of the article, it was emphasized that
the point was to reintegrate them into the common law. Thus, they
are "*removable after 3 years and their appointment will be carried out
in the same way as the other officers of the G.O.*"[15] In a magnanimous
gesture, the Grand Master himself would offer to renounce his irre-
movability and also be subject to election every three years, but the
Brothers refused.

For the vote to be fair, it had to be done in full knowledge of the
facts, so during the 122nd assembly of the Grand Orient[16]—February 15, 1782—it was decided after the debates that all deputies of
the lodges would be able to ask for disclosures from the secretariat
of the Grand Orient. Also, all the members would have access to
the files, as long as they were commissioned by a lodge. It was also
decided that, as far as possible, agendas would always be announced
ahead of time. One subject that would occupy the bodies of the association for a long time was the establishment of a specific procedure for electing the officers of the different chambers. Indeed, they
were the ones who, with the assistance of the secretariat, ensured
the daily administration of the Grand Orient, which indicates the
importance of the challenge. In August 1785, the voting procedure
was presented in great detail:

> "*The first expert shall count the voters and shall give to each
> a ballot. Each voter shall write on this ballot the name, sur-
> name, statuses, age, and residence of the brother he believes*

---

15 FM¹ 98, folio 11, back.

16 122nd assembly of the G∴O∴, February 15, 1782, BnF FM¹ 16, folio 186,
back.

should be nominated. The first expert shall collect the bal-
lots. The Brothers who have no one to nominate shall sub-
mit blank ballots. The ballots shall be given to the President
who shall count them in the presence of two experts. If the
number of ballots is not equal to the number of voters, the
operation shall begin again. The President shall open the
ballots and shall read what they contain. The ballots that
nominate the same names shall be gathered and there shall
be as many stacks as there are different names. Each stack
shall be counted and the President shall appoint all the
Brothers nominated beginning with the one who received
the most votes...."[17]

Is this not an example of the learning process of democracy? Several other examples of procedural votes of this kind can be found in the internal rules of the Grand Orient. But we should be wary of models that seem too perfect. While they focus much attention on the rigor of the elective procedure, the managers of the Grand Orient simultaneously try to limit access to the offices by introducing some measure of cooptation. This raises the opposition of the Brother Desjunquières who argues against:

"...the rule of August 17, 1785 [which] tends to complete-
ly separate the officers of the Grand Orient from the depu-
ties of the lodges and make it a distinct body. I have never
considered the Grand Orient except as the lodge of deputies
who have the right to elect from within it, officers to preside
over, conduct, and clarify the work, as well as administrate
more specifically the Order's affairs and prepare the docu-
ments to be brought before the G. O."[18]

Tellingly, the examples he then gives to legitimize respect for the democratic spirit are classic cases of the most traditional social practices of the *Ancien* Régime:

---

17 Archives of the GODF, BnF FM^1 16, folio 246.
18 Archives of the GODF, BnF FM^1 16, folio 247.

"If we want to take civil societies as a model, nothing exists any longer or nothing comparable is practiced unless we look to the first finance companies or to the latest corporations of arts and crafts."

This shows how the connections between traditional and new social practices were more complex than the simple opposition of ancient and modern! Brother Desjunquière's argument won the day and the rule that had been approved was annulled. All the deputies from the lodges at the Grand Orient became again eligible for the various offices. What is interesting about this episode is that it illustrates the complexity of the development of this new democratic social practice and also shows how it is connected to older forms of social relationships. The 15 years between the formation of the Grand Orient and 1789 would witness several similar episodes. In each case, the details of the debates, the constant back and forth between the various bodies, and the frequent repetitions all make the reading of these long minutes particularly tedious. Nevertheless, our hope is that eighteenth-century specialists will take note of how relevant the documentation contained in the archives of the Grand Orient of France is for the study of the formation of democratic social practices in the years preceding the Revolution.

During the early days of 1789, the Grand Orient sent a circular to all the lodges it corresponded with to report on its activity. The introduction of this text is particularly interesting. It reads:

"Enlightened concerning their true interests, the LL∴ felt it necessary to be governed in a uniform way, and to submit to rules drawn from the very essence of their association: this motive led them to unite to form a common center, and they decreed that the body that would regulate them would be composed of their representatives; therefore, they attributed legislative power to this body, and established it as judge of their differences.

The constitution of the G∴O∴, VV∴DD∴BB∴, is thus purely democratic: nothing shall be decided except accord-

ing to the will of the LLs∴, brought before the General Assemblies by their representatives."[19]

Of course, the general atmosphere that began to affect French society at the beginning of 1789 may not be entirely absent from what was written here; but it can clearly be concluded that this text was in line with what had been the doctrine of the Grand Orient since 1773.

---

19 Circular of the 19th day of the eleventh month 5788 (January 19, 1789).

Theophilanthropy: A (Masonic) Plan for a Religion without Legends

C an deism be the object of worship? This was the ambition of Theophilanthropy, a movement that is largely forgotten today but which, for almost two years from 18 Fructidor year V (September 4, 1797) to 30 Prairial year VII (June 18, 1799), was practically the "official religion" of France. In the beginning, it was no more than a strange utopist project, like several others that existed during the Revolution. But the political situation and the protection of one of the strong men of the revolutionary government, the "Director" La Révellière-Lépeaux, brought it to center stage. After tracing the main paths of this curious story,[1] we will investigate the principals professed by the Theophilanthropists, and then explore the numerous links with Freemasonry.

The Origin and History of a New Religion

In 1796, Chemin fils, a young and relatively obscure bookseller, published a plan for deist worship entitled *Manuel des Théoanthropophiles*. He was not the first but, to his great surprise, the book achieved a certain success and he found several enthusiastic readers who pressed him to move on from the plan to the organization of a small circle that would put into practice the deist worship outlined in the work. Some of the enlightened bourgeoisie, such as the bene-

---

1 The history of Theophilanthropy has been magisterially traced by the great historian of the French Revolution, Albert Mathiez, in a landmark thesis that remains, more than a century after its publication, the essential work of reference. We rely in part on this study, which we use extensively: Albert Mathiez, *La Théophilanthropie et le culte décadaire 1796-1801, Essai sur l'histoire religieuse de la Révolution*, Paris, Félix Alcan, 1903, reprinted by Slatkine Reprints, Genève, 1975. One may also consult: Jean-Pierre Chantin, "Les adeptes de la théophilanthropie, pour une autre lecture d'Albert Mathiez," in *Rives méditerranéennes*, No. 14 (2003) Révolution et minorités religieuses, pp. 63-73.

factor of the blind Valentin Haüy or the deputy Goupil de Prefelne, gathered with their families in the little Church of St. Catherine to celebrate the Father of Nature and to teach each other the purest of morals. They also slightly changed the name proposed by Chemin to "Theophilanthropists," which better suited their tastes. Then, what could have remained as an astonishing experience moved, thanks to the political situation, into the grand narrative of history. In 1797, the leaders of the Directory were faced with the slow revival of conservative and monarchist opinion in the country. The "refractory priests" were at the forefront of this opposition to the Republic. Moreover, as men of the eighteenth century, the republicans were convinced that politics and religion were intimately linked, and that revolution in the political domain must be accompanied by grand changes in the religious sphere. This opinion can be found not only among Robespierre's disciples, but also among practically all of the supporters of the Revolution, even the most moderate. Thus, that Egeria of the liberals, Madame de Staël, could write:

> The system of the French Republic can only be based on the total acceptance of reason as the foundation for all institutions and all ideas . . . All religion that has as its foundation what we call dogmas, which is to say mysteries, and which rest on blind faith, all religions of this type are of necessity based on the same arguments which, applied in a different context, hold up the nobility and the monarchy.[2]

Catholicism is inextricably linked to the Monarchy, and if the Republic wishes to build a durable foundation, it must rely on a religious revolution. This was the subject of a great speech made by Director La Révellière-Lépeaux at the Institute—the temple of republican thought—on 12 Floréal of Year V (1 May 1797). Heirs to the Girondins, the men of the Directory were "moderate republicans, though their republicanism was not moderate."[3] Despite the

---

2   *Des circonstances actuelles qui peuvent terminer la Révolution et des principes qui doivent fonder la République en France* (1798), Editions Fischbacher, Paris, 1906, p. 220. Quoted by Mathiez, *op. cit.,* pp. 267-268.

3   This phrase apparently comes from Waldeck-Rousseau. Historians apply it to

aversion they might have felt for Robespierre and the failure of the cult of the Supreme Being, the establishment of the Republic did not seem possible to them unless accompanied by the advent of a new religion that would plant in the hearts of citizens the ideas and morals of the Republic. The picture of the religion that La Révellière deemed necessary in order to establish the moral unity of the French people coincided broadly with the new faith professed by the small group of Theophilanthropists. Thus the group was thrust into the spotlight. Montesquieu had shown that the Republic was based on virtue, and the new religion would teach that virtue to the people.

> The cult of the Theophilanthropists arose in an era when a faction hostile to the Republic was threatening France with violent disturbance. Also [...] a religious institution based on philosophical principles tended by its nature to strengthen the Republican government.[4]

As a result of the fame that La Révellière-Lépeaux's great speech had assured them, the Theophilanthropists would soon draw a whole crowd of new devotees, many of them sincere and others aware of the almost official protection granted by the government. The coup d'état of 18 Fructidor Year V (September 4, 1797) made La Révellière-Lépeaux—whose name has now fallen into obscurity—the leading figure of the regime. The political success of its protector promoted the development of the new religion in the country. In Paris, almost 18 places of Theophilanthropic worship were established in several churches, renamed appropriately: Temple of the Reunion (Saint-Merri), Temple of the Social Contract (Saint-Eustache), Temple of Fidelity (Saint-Gervais), Temple of Concord (Saint-Sulpice), etc. The chronicle of the allocation of different churches to the Theophilanthropists and the controversies that this provoked is a whole separate, and often comical, side of their history. Theophilanthropist groups were established in many

---

the liberal republicans of the Third Republican, which in some ways the men of the Directorate preceded.

4 *Qu'est-ce que la Théophilanthropie?* p. 16.

provincial towns. Protected and favored by the government, the church experienced sustained growth for almost two years. For the most part, however, the fall of its defender La Révellière-Lépeaux in the coup d'état of 30 Prairial Year VII (June 18, 1799) marked the end of the adventure. To everyone's surprise, however, Theophilanthropy survived this heavy blow and, despite the suspicion it aroused due to its links with the ousted government, remained very active in Paris and in the provinces. It would not disappear until the Concordat of 1801, when the papal negotiators made its suppression a condition of the agreement with the First Consul.

Simple and Practical Principles

As he himself said in his *Manuel des Théophilanthropes* (1797), Chemin had done no more than to set down on paper the doctrine of the "natural religion." This holds to two principles, or "dogmas" in the language of the era:

> "Theophilanthropists believe in the existence of God and in the immortality of the soul. The wonder of the universe attests to the existence of a first being. The faculty we have for thought assures us that we ourselves have a principle superior to matter which will survive the dissolution of our bodies. The existence of God and the immortality of the soul do not require long demonstrations; they are the truths of feelings that each of us has in his heart."[5]

As truths of feelings, the two dogmas of Theophilanthropy had another essential justification in the eyes of the new church—they were useful:

> Theophilanthropists hold yet more firmly to this double belief because it is as necessary to the preservation of so-

---

5   *Manuel des Théophilanthropes ou adorateurs de Dieu et amis des hommes contenant l'exposition de leurs dogmes, de leur morale et de leurs pratiques religieuses, avec une instruction sur l'organisation et la célébration du Culte*, second edition, L'Abeille, Paris, An V-1797, pp. 11-12.

ciety as to the happiness of the individual.[6]

Good is everything that tends to preserve man or perfect him. Evil is everything that tends to degrade man or deteriorate him.

There are no good acts except those which are useful.[7]

Principles are true when they are useful, but also when they are simple. The revealed religions have obscured their primitive simplicity by encumbering the principles with "theological" myths and "sacerdotal" customs. At times the Theophilanthropists thought to call themselves "primitive Christians," as they believed that they professed the original faith. This idea of a "natural religion" dominated the second part of the eighteenth century and the first two thirds of the nineteenth century. For the "philosophes," the different revealed religions all derived from this primitive religion which the priests had sadly overloaded with useless dogmas and obscure myths in order to legitimize the "priesthood." This thesis would be defended and promoted by a book—in fact ten volumes riddled with Latin—that would long resonate in men's minds: *L'Origine de tous les Cultes ou Religion Universelle* by Dupuis. The author was already a renowned intellectual at the end of the Ancien Régime, but he had to wait for the Revolution before he could publish his impious theories, and his magnum opus did not appear until 1794.[8] The Theophilanthropists wanted to rediscover and revive this "principal," by which they meant primitive and universal, religion:

There are many faiths and they may have within them infinite variations, but there cannot be but one sole religion, the universal religion.[9]

---

6   *Manuel des Théophilanthropes..., op. cit.,* p. 12.

7   *Manuel des Théophilanthropes..., op. cit.,* p. 19.

8   *Origine de tous les Cultes ou Religion Universelle* by Dupuis, Citizen of France, in Paris, with H. Agasse, Year III of the Republic, one and indivisble.

9   *Qu'est-ce que la Théophilanthropie? op. cit.,* p. 32.

With their feeling, their utility and their simplicity, the Theophilanthropists were the loyal sons of Rousseau and Voltaire. Due to the value they ascribed to simplicity and their allergy to "theological trickery" typical of eighteenth-century philosophy, it is therefore quite difficult to go much further into the doctrine of the Theophilanthropists. When a Protestant society invited them to reveal the detail of their "confession of faith," Chemin replied that this would:

> require a theological discussion and in consequence draw me beyond both my personal principles and those of Theophilanthropy.[10]

Moreover:

> What God is, what the soul is, how God rewards the good and punishes the evil, these are questions beyond the scope of the Theophilanthropists' inquiries. They are convinced that there is too much distance between God and his creation for his creation to pretend to known Him.[11]

Finally, the "philosophical" claims of Theophilanthropy touched more on the moral and social ideas it professed than on its religious concepts. For the Theophilanthropists, the idea of God was more sentimental, literary, and poetic than truly theological. To grasp it, one should consider Voltaire's Prayer or take as one's guide Victor Hugo in the admirable tenth chapter of *Les Misérables* entitled "The Bishop in the Presence of an Unknown Light." The good priest Bienvenu braves the condemnation of Bourbon Restoration society by going to visit in his final moments G., a former member of the National Convention. They fall into conversation and, sensing his end approaching:

---

10 *Qu'est-ce que la Théophilanthropie? ou mémoire contenant l'origine et l'histoire de cette institution; ses rapports avec le Christianisme et l'aperçu de l'influence qu'elle peut avoir sur tous les cultes, en réponse aux questions posées par la Société Teylerienne de Harlem (en Hollande)*, 2nd edition, Paris, La Libre Conscience, 1868, p. 23.

11 *Manuel des Théophilanthropes..., op. cit.*, p. 13.

The former representative of the people made no reply. He was seized with a fit of trembling. He looked towards heaven, and in his glance a tear gathered slowly. When the eyelid was full, the tear trickled down his livid cheek, and he said, almost in a stammer, quite low, and to himself, while his eyes were plunged in the depths:—

"O thou! O ideal! Thou alone existest!"

The Bishop experienced an indescribable shock.

After a pause, the old man raised a finger heavenward and said:—

"The infinite is. He is there. If the infinite had no person, person would be without limit; it would not be infinite; in other words, it would not exist. There is, then, an I. That I of the infinite is God."

But in passing from theory into practice, in experimenting with the establishment of a genuine faith, the leaders of the young Church would discover that it is not always easy to hold onto simplicity of principles. Certainly:

To adore God is above all to obey his law, which he has clearly explained to us via that internal feeling that carries us towards good and turns us away from evil, and which we call our conscience.[12]

Moreover, the Theophilanthropists "*do not attach any superstitious importance to external practices*" and "*they consider their faith not as a tribute which God has need of, but as a means of moral education and fraternal reunion.*"[13] In the beginning, the organization of the faith was effectively going to be very simple:

Some moral inscriptions, a simple altar on which they lay, as a symbol of their gratitude for the Creator's blessings,

---

12 *Manuel des Théophilanthropes..., op. cit.*, p. 18.

13 *Qu'est-ce que la Théophilanthropie? op. cit.*, p. 25.

some flowers or some fruits depending on the season, and a rostrum for lectures and discussion—that is all the ornamentation of their Temples.[14]

"A paterfamilias, properly and simply dressed and bare-headed, gives readings of the first two chapters from this manual about their dogmas and morality, and of a paragraph on the day-to-day conduct of the Theophilanthropists.

After this reading ... [he] recites aloud the prayer Father of Nature

The attendants repeat in the same manner in low voices.

They sit to hear lectures or moral discussions which accord with the principles of ... religions, of benevolence and of universal tolerance [...].

These lectures or discussions are interspersed with song.[15]

At the same time, however, the legitimate concern to make the faith better organized and more attractive, and the necessity of highlighting—and even symbolically rewarding—some people's engagement in the life of the Church led to an enrichment of the Theophilanthropist liturgy that would cause debate. Controversy would notably form around the question of the "priesthood." For the philosophers of the eighteenth century, priests were one of the plagues on all civilizations. They had invented the idea of a priesthood in order to ensure their power over the people, while God naturally had no need of intermediaries between himself and men. A philosophical religion, as Theophilanthropy wished to be, should therefore not have priests. In the beginning, worship was led only by a "Paterfamilias," chosen almost randomly or appointed by turn, whose costume was limited to being *properly and simply dressed and bare-headed.*" Naturally, however, the conduct of the ceremony

---

14 *Manuel des Théophilanthropes..., op. cit.,* p. 33.

15 *Manuel des Théophilanthropes..., op. cit.,* pp. 36-37.

and the choice and explanation of texts presented to the faithful required particular skills and, after several months, the Church saw the emergence of personalities who took control of the office of "Paterfamilias" and who began to be called "Readers" and "Orators." Soon after, the celebrant was assigned a particular uniform, which echoed others:

> considering that all men who fulfill a serious function should have a corresponding appearance, and desiring that its readers and orators appear in garments that are always equally simple, neat and decent, it was thought that they could have, for religious and moral celebrations, a particular costume that would consist of a long habit of a single color. The color white was adopted as it was a symbol of the simplicity and purity of Theophilanthropic principles.[16]

Some months later, the clothing of the celebrants would see a further advance in sophistication and symbolism:

> It is thought that, so that readers might appear in garments that are always equally simple, neat and decent, it would be good that they should have, for their public engagements, a particular costume that would consist of a sky-blue tunic, stretching from the collar down to the feet, with a pink belt and a white robe over it, open in front.[17]

At the same time, the Church's liturgy became richer, as can be seen from successive editions, as did, augmented and enriched each time by Chemin, the Theophilanthropic reference books that appeared under the titles *Manuals, Worship, Rituals, The Religious*

---

16 [Jean-Baptiste Chemin], *Le Culte des Théophilanthropes ou adorateurs de Dieu et amis des hommes contenant leur manuel, leur catéchisme et recueil de discours, Lectures, Hymnes et Cantiques pour toutes leurs fêtes religieuses et morales*, third edition, J. Decker, Bâle, 1798, note 1, p. 9.

17 J.B. Chemin, *Rituel des Théophilanthropes, contenant l'ordre de leurs différents exercices et le Recueil des Cantiques, Hymnes et Odes adoptés dans les différents Temples tant à Paris que des départements...* Paris, An VI (1798), note 1, p. 4.

Year, etc. As a "natural" religion, Theophilanthropy regulated its calendar according to the seasons of the cosmos and of human life. Thus it developed ceremonies to celebrate the milestones of the year (the solstices and equinoxes) with the *Festivals of Spring, of Summer, of Autumn* and *of Winter*[18] and the milestones of life (birth, adolescence, marriage, death, etc.).

Even if you want to stick to simple principles, when religious ideas are developed into a faith, the need for a symbolic apparatus arises.

Theophilanthropy and Freemasonry

In his thesis, Mathiez made a direct link between Theophilanthropy and Freemasonry. He even saw in Theophilanthropy *"an overt Masonry."*[19] For him, Chemin was certainly a Mason, and he put many of the principles and practices of the lodges into his new religion. The question is complex because, in fact, Chemin was not just a Mason, but a very active Mason. However, his known masonic activity took place under the Bourbon Restoration and the July Monarchy, and there is no proof whatsoever that he had already been initiated during the Revolution. It should be remembered nonetheless that there were numerous initiations during the revolutionary period which the circumstances did not permit to be recorded in writing. The lodges waited for more peaceful times, around 1800, before returning to the keeping of records and tables. One indication, meanwhile, that suggests Chemin was not initiated in the era of Theophilanthropy is that he cannot be found either in the tables of lodges under the Empire. In fact, he does not appear until 1818 in the Lodge of Trinosophes. However, we do not know when he was initiated because his entry into the Trinosophes was an affiliation. It therefore remains possible—but in our view unlikely—that he had been accepted as a Mason at the beginning of the Revolution and that, for various reasons, he had not been

---

18 One can find the details of the "liturgical calendar" of the Theophilanthropists and the rituals and readings suggested for the different ceremonies in *Le Culte des Théophilanthropes...,* op. cit., Bâle 1778.

19 Albert Mathiez, *op. cit.,* p. 83.

active in Freemasonry under the Empire until he was affiliated to the Trinosophes in 1818. In any case, whether Chemin was or was not a Mason is ultimately of secondary importance, as the principles of Freemasonry were almost in the public domain at the time, and there were certainly quite a number of Masons in the story of Theophilanthropy.

While the two principles of Theophilanthropy—the existence of God and the immortality of the soul – are drawn directly from the Deism of the Enlightenment, they also have much older traditional religious sources. In fact, these two ideas are often associated with, for example, the Noahides, those sages of Antiquity who revered the precepts given by God to Noah.[20] Anderson's Constitutions reference the Noahides in order to anchor the origins of Freemasonry. Equally, in Paris in the years preceding the Revolution, the *Philalèthes* of the famous Loge des *Amis Réunis* saw in these two principles the pinnacle of masonic ideas.[21] If at the time Chemin had had no personal contact with Freemasonry whether directly or by proxy through friends (which, it must be said, would be truly astonishing)—this man of letters could have discovered it through numerous works. Note, for example, that at the beginning of the Revolution, there appeared a pamphlet which divulged in detail the rituals of a masonic Deist system which showed numerous features shared with Theophilanthropy: The Elect of Truth. Originally, The Elect of Truth was a system of high degrees established by the Masons of Rennes in 1770.[22] The system then won a certain amount of success and was disseminated in several towns in the west and in

---

20 See, for example, the article devoted to them in the *Encyclopédie* of Diderot and d'Alembert: "*Noahides ... The precepts given to this patriarch and his children seem to be no more than the precepts of the natural rights ... to adore the creator* [they must] *inspire the sentiments of humanity in all our behavior. Encyclopédie ou Dictionnaire raisonné...*, Genève, Pellet, 1778, Volume 23, p. 5.

21 "Première Circulaire..." in: Charles Porset, *Les Philalèthes et les Convents de Paris, une politique de la folie*, Honoré Champion, Paris, 1996, pp. 262-263.

22 See: Pierre Mollier, "Un système rationaliste de Hauts-grades au XVIIIe siècle : Les Elus de la Vérité ", in *Studia latomorum & historica-Mélanges offerts à Daniel Ligou*, collected by Charles Porset, Honoré Champion, 1998, pp. 313-326.

Paris. At the top degree of the system, the Elect of Truth professed a militant Voltarian Deism—which is to say a rational Deism extremely hostile to revealed religions. As a testimony of the time also affirms: "These notebooks were divulged and publicly sold during the revolution and served as the basis for the religious faith that the republic has adopted."[23]

But if Freemasonry did probably play a role in the origins and the history of Theophilanthropy, it was above all in the new faith's afterlife that it would have a major presence. Somehow, once forbidden, Theophilanthropy would take refuge in the lodges. Chemin-Dupontès became a masonic luminary, and even a luminary of the Ancient and Accepted Scottish Rite. Thus he was the author, in 1823 of a memoir entitled *Mémoire sur l'Écossisme par le F∴ Chemin-Dupontès G:. Inspecteur Général du Rit Écossais, Député au G∴ Orient de France, Vénérable de la R∴L∴ des Sept Écossais Réunis et auteur de l'Encyclopédie maçonnique*. After twenty years, he would graft into Freemasonry many of the ideas of the revolutionary religion:

> The initiated, reborn into a new life, recognized that many teachers ∴, and he himself perhaps, had allowed themselves to be led by two opposing errors ... a lack of faith ... or a superstitious faith. He freely adopted the enlightened faith that the initiation presented him with, this simple and reasoned faith that makes him recognize his relations with his creator and with his peers ... encourages him in the practice of all public and private virtues.[24]

During the Revolution, the citizens of Strasbourg had practiced the new faiths "with gravity and conviction."[25] In 1827, an Alsacien Mason, Brother Riebesthal, published a curious pamphlet entitled *Rituel maçonnique pour tous les rites* [*Masonic Rituals for All Cere-*

---

23 *Idem*, p. 324.

24 *Cours pratique de Franc-maçonnerie publié sur la demande et sous les auspices de la R \ L \ Isis-Montyon*, by F \C \Dupontès, third section, degree of Master, Paris, 1841, p. 182.

25 Albert Mathiez, *op. cit.*, pp. 491-492.

monies].*²⁶* It is a surprise to discover their rituals for conducting *The Festival of the Revival of Nature at the spring equinox, The Festival of the Triumph of Light at the summer solstice, The Festival of Nature's Rest at the autumn equinox,* and *The Festival of the Regeneration of Light at the winter solstice.* Nature, regeneration—the very titles of these festivals, completely unknown in eighteenth century Freemasonry, of course recall the religious experiments of the Revolution.*²⁷* This association and the religious orientation that it suggests are confirmed in two other rituals explained by Riebesthal: the "Masonic Baptism of a Lowton (at under three years of age)," and the "Confirmation of a Lowton (who has reached the age of seventeen)." Finally, the work concludes with a list of "Common holidays during the year" which also unavoidably recalls the republican calendar and Theophilanthropy. Each of the 52 Sundays of the year has been assigned a moral or philosophical theme as part of a Festival of Honor, of Sincerity, of Brotherly Love, of Wisdom, of Patriotism, of Candor, of Reason, of Patience, of Mercy, and of Concord. Riebesthal explains that these ceremonies are aimed at:

> better experiencing the effect and feeling the advantage of the reasonable, natural and purely moral faith that Freemasonry should profess*²⁸* [...] The ceremonies that it employs and the emblems with which it adorns its temples have the goal of inspiring man with the most pure morality, of interesting him in the good of humanity, of revealing to him the truth and of making him attentive to the phenomena of nature, to lift his soul and urge him to contemplate the night sky where myriad stars in their resplendent light announce to him and prove to him the existence of

---

26   Ch.-G. Riebesthal, *Rituel maçonnique pour tous les rites*, Strasbourg, Silbermann, s.d. [1826].

27   See: Pierre Mollier, "Chrétien-Guillaume Riebesthal: Des religions de la Révolution aux cérémonies paramaçonniques " in *Les Frères Réunis à Strasbourg, une loge maçonnique engagée*, catalog of the exhibition presented at the History Museum of the City of Strasbourg from October 15, 2011 to February 5, 2012, ID Edition, 2011, pp. 43-47.

28   Ch.-G. Riebestal, *op. cit.*, p. 8.

the incomprehensible Being who possesses the ultimate in power, in grandeur, and in all the perfections.[29]

These words trace almost verbatim the maxims of Theophilanthropy. It should be no surprise, then, that the Paris correspondent of Brother Riebesthal and his Strasbourg Lodges was Brother Chemin-Dupontès. These para-masonic ceremonies, which were all the rage in the nineteenth century and are still sometimes practiced today—"adoption" or "masonic baptism," "conjugal recognition" or "masonic marriage," "funereal handling" or "masonic obsequies"—are in origin directly descended from Theophilanthropy. From the aftermath of the Revolution and up until 1877, the Grand Orient de France considered Freemasonry as the incarnation of natural religion and considered itself a deist church. In some cases, consciously and for the most part unconsciously, it presented itself as the continuation of Theophilanthropy. And 1877 did not mark, as it is sometimes suggested, a break with traditional Judeo-Christian Freemasonry, but a handover from the older generation professing the rational deism of Voltaire and the Revolution, to the new generation of the 1860s, who were disciples of the rational agnosticism of Auguste Comte.

Theophilanthropy had wanted to be a religion reduced to the essential principles of the religious. Freemasonry of the nineteenth century was profoundly marked by the religious heritage of the Revolution, and for many it certainly was—at that time at least—a religion reduced to principles.

The last of the Theophilanthropists were still trying to gather for their worship on 20 Vendémiaire Year X (October 12, 1801). By order of the government, they were forbidden access to their temples and asked to disperse. After some protestation and vain attempts at approaching the First Consul, who had at one time been quite closely linked to La Revellière-Lépeaux, the purest cult of the natural religion was buried in obscurity. The Theophilanthropists preached tolerance. They proclaimed from the pulpit—professing this religion on which all men could agree—that they were friends

---

29 Ch.-G. Riebestal, *op. cit.*, Preface, p. VIII.

to all faiths. They were nonetheless considered, by deeply Catholic France, as the religious arm of the Revolution and the enemy to be defeated. The historic episode of Theophilanthropy may seem picturesque and anecdotal, but it nonetheless reveals structural elements of the religious and political history of our country. While in Great Britain and the Anglo-Saxon world, deism fits into the continuity of Christianity and appears as a prolonged Unitarianism, in France both in the domain of ideas and in the domain of history, deism is a break with Christianity and clearly fits into the critical camp of rationalism and the Enlightenment. It is probably this philosophical and religious context that explains in part the evolution of Freemasonry in the final third of the nineteenth century.

CHAPTER XII

APPENDIX 1

Voltaire's Prayer[30]

So it is no longer to men that I address myself, it is to you, God of all beings, of all worlds and of all times. If it is permitted for weak creatures lost in the vastness and imperceptible to the rest of the universe to dare to demand anything of you, you who have given everything, you whose decrees are as immutable as they are eternal, then deign to look with pity on the mistakes attached to our nature, and do not let these mistakes become our calamities. You have not given us a heart to hate ourselves, or hands to kill ourselves. Make it so that we mutually aid each other to bear the burden of a painful and transitory life; that the small differences in the clothes which cover our foolish bodies, in all our inadequate languages, in all our ridiculous customs, in all our imperfect laws, in all our senseless opinions, in all our conditions so disproportionate in our eyes, and so equal before you; that all these little nuances that distinguish these atoms known as men be not the signals for hate and for persecution; that those who light candles in broad daylight to worship you tolerate those who are content with the light of your sun; that those who cover their dress in white cloth to show that we must love you not hate those who say the same thing under a coat of black wool; that it be the same to adore you in a dialect formed from an ancient language or in a dialect more modern; that those whose dress is colored red or purple, and who rule over a little parcel of a little heap of the mud of this world, and who possess a few round pieces of a certain metal, enjoy without pride that which they call grandeur and wealth, and that the others watch them without envy, for you know that in these vanities there is nothing to envy, nor to be proud of.

Let all men remember that they are brothers! Let them hold in horror tyranny exercised over souls, as they hold in contempt the banditry that seizes by force the fruits of peaceful labor and industry! If the scourges

---

30 Voltaire, *Traité sur la tolérance à l'occasion de la mort de Jean Calas* (1763), extract from Chapter XXIII.

of war are inevitable, let us not hate one another in the bosom of peace, and let us use the brief moment of our existence to praise in a thousand different languages, from Siam to California, your kindness which has given us this moment.

APPENDIX 2

The invocation of the Father of Nature is the principal prayer of the Theophilanthropists[31]:

> *Father of nature, I bless your kindnesses and I thank you for your gifts.*
>
> *I admire the beautiful order of things that you have established in your wisdom and that you maintain with your providence, and I submit myself forever to this universal order.*
>
> *I do not ask you for the power to do good. For you have given me this power and, along with it, conscience to love good, reason to understand it, and liberty to choose it. I would not then have any excuse if I were to do evil. I make before you the commitment to use my freedom only in order to do good, no matter what attractions evil might seem to offer.*
>
> *I will never address indiscreet prayers to you. You know the creatures that have come from your hand, their needs no more escape your eyes than do their most secret thoughts. I pray only that you redress the mistakes of the world and my own mistakes, for almost all the evils that afflict men come from their mistakes.*
>
> *Full of confidence in your justice and in your kindness, I resign myself to whatever comes, my sole wish being that your will be done.*

---

31 *Manuel des Théophilanthropes..., op. cit.*, pp. 29-31.

Related Titles from Westphalia Press

A Place in the Lodge: Dr. Rob Morris, Freemasonry and the Order of the Eastern Star
by Nancy Stearns Theiss, PhD

Ridiculed as "petticoat masonry," critics of the Order of the Eastern Star did not deter Rob Morris' goal to establish a Masonic organization that included women as members. Morris carried the ideals of Freemasonry through a despairing time of American history.

Brought to Light: The Mysterious George Washington Masonic Cave
by Jason Williams MD

The George Washington Masonic Cave near Charles Town, West Virginia, contains a signature carving of George Washington dated 1748. This book painstakingly pieces together the chronicled events and real estate archives related to the cavern in order to sort out fact from fiction.

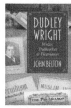

Dudley Wright: Writer, Truthseeker & Freemason
by John Belton

Dudley Wright (1868-1950) was an Englishman and professional journalist who took a universalist approach to the various great Truths of Life. He travelled though many religions in his life and wrote about them all, but was probably most at home with Islam.

History of the Grand Orient of Italy
Emanuela Locci, Editor

No book in Masonic literature upon the history of Italian Freemasonry has been edited in English up to now. This work consists of eight studies, covering a span from the Eighteenth Century to the end of the WWII, tracing through the story, the events and pursuits related to the Grand Orient of Italy.

The Great Transformation: Scottish Freemasonry 1725-1810
by Dr. Mark C. Wallace

This book examines Scottish Freemasonry in its wider British and European contexts between the years 1725 and 1810. The Enlightenment effectively crafted the modern mason and propelled Freemasonry into a new era marked by growing membership and the creation of the Grand Lodge of Scotland.

Getting the Third Degree: Fraternalism, Freemasonry and History
Edited by Guillermo De Los Reyes and Paul Rich

As this engaging collection demonstrates, the doors being opened on the subject range from art history to political science to anthropology, as well as gender studies, sociology and more. The organizations discussed may insist on secrecy, but the research into them belies that.

Freemasonry: A French View
by Roger Dachez and Alain Bauer

Perhaps one should speak not of Freemasonry but of Freemasonries in the plural. In each country Masonic historiography has developed uniqueness. Two of the best known French Masonic scholars present their own view of the worldwide evolution and challenging mysteries of the fraternity over the centuries.

Worlds of Print: The Moral Imagination of an Informed Citizenry, 1734 to 1839
by John Slifko

John Slifko argues that freemasonry was representative and played an important role in a larger cultural transformation of literacy and helped articulate the moral imagination of an informed democratic citizenry via fast emerging worlds of print.

Why Thirty-Three?: Searching for Masonic Origins
by S. Brent Morris, PhD

What "high degrees" were in the United States before 1830? What were the activities of the Order of the Royal Secret, the precursor of the Scottish Rite? A complex organization with a lengthy pedigree like Freemasonry has many basic foundational questions waiting to be answered, and that's what this book does: answers questions.

Made in the USA
Coppell, TX
11 July 2023

19003036R00095